Understanding Supervision and the PhD

Also available from Continuum

Dr Dr I Feel Like . . . Doing a PhD, Lucy Russell

Continuum Guide to Successful Teaching in Higher Education,
  Manuel Martinez-Pons

The Future of Higher Education, Les Bell, Howard Stevenson, Michael Neary

Understanding Supervision and the PhD

Moira Peelo

continuum

Continuum International Publishing Group

The Tower Building   80 Maiden Lane
11 York Road   Suite 704
London SE1 7NX   New York, NY 10038

www.continuumbooks.com

British Library Cataloguing-in-Publication Data
A catalogue record for this book is available from the British Library.

ISBN: 978-1-4411-7754-4 (paperback)
ISBN: 978-1-4411-0449-6 (hardcover)

Library of Congress Cataloging-in-Publication Data
Peelo, Moira T.
  Understanding supervision and the PhD / Moira Peelo.
    p. cm.
  Includes bibliographical references.
  ISBN: 978-1-4411-0449-6 (hardcover)
  ISBN: 978-1-4411-7754-4 (pbk.)
  1. Graduate students–Supervision of–United States. 2. Doctoral
  students–United States. I. Title.

  LB2371.4.P44 2010
  378.1'794–dc22

                                        2010014787

Typeset by Newgen Imaging Systems Pvt Ltd, Chennai, India
Printed and bound in India by Replika Press Pvt Ltd

Contents

Part 4 **DEVELOPMENT AND TRAINING**

Introduction

As this book neared completion, newspapers were reporting that universities face large and immediate cuts in government funding: these have been announced at the last minute and come on top of cuts already planned (see, for example, Grimston, 2010). Their precise impact has yet to be seen, but academic jobs were already under threat before the newest cuts were added into the mix. This stop-start funding has been seen before, and universities have changed and changed again in response to successive funding initiatives since the 1960s. But in spite of all the massive changes that have occurred in higher education, political rhetoric continues to cast universities as rich and leisurely places. Doctoral students, like all students, will not be immune to changes in universities resulting from cuts in budgets and these will come on top of what, in the last ten years, has been a period of accelerated change in research education.

For researchers into higher education, the task is to try to represent the actuality of a diverse higher education sector; for practitioners like myself, engaged in providing courses for supervisors and research students, the task is to try to influence academic practices within the reality of the educational context. In part, influencing practice requires unpicking what the experience is. Doctoral education has long ceased to be a leisurely and indulged form of extended scholarship (if it truly ever was this). Reflecting the changes in universities, doctoral research education has been subject to successive reports, changing modes of funding and competing assumptions and expectations about what should happen and what should be provided. How do supervisors manage the pressures produced by these changes? How do students adjust to the experience of doctoral education in such a rapidly changing landscape? Most importantly, how do both supervisors and students develop and learn their crafts?

This book is about supervision and the PhD in universities in the UK. It draws on my life: as a researcher, as a student, as a teacher, as a writer and, more recently working at the boundaries of what are now called 'educational' and 'learning' development activities. That means that I both provide training courses for supervisors and support student development and performance. I have drawn substantially from my own research and scholarship and that of others; however, the thread that joins disparate pictures of what supervising the PhD can look like is my interpretation of the varied fragments that make up this account of supervision and the PhD in the UK. It is not a book that tells people how to supervise (in the traditional sense), but I hope it will be used by supervisors who wish to extend and develop their repertoire of supervisory skills.

My own relationship with the PhD as an educational experience was not a good one, and since getting my doctorate many years ago I have worked with students struggling with intellectual growth and with supervisors. It has been easy to accept the dichotomy that academe is divided into good supervisors and bad supervisors; bad supervisors and their students face problems while good ones do not. Obviously, such simple assumptions could not withstand the impact of data collected from both supervisors and students. I assume now that difficult problems occur in all supervision, and what distinguishes better from worse are the ways in which problems are managed – especially in supervisors' levels of professionalism and humanity.

My current view is easy to summarize: that the PhD is a risky enterprise for both supervisors and students; and while bad supervisors exist and make life miserable for everyone, good supervisors, who also exist, do not guarantee successful completion of the PhD or a straightforward journey. The PhD is not a uniform degree, and supervision is not a clear-cut, simple activity; students study part time, at a distance from their universities, on doctoral programmes and in the workplace. Then there are some who study full time while fully funded and resident at their place of study. Further, data analysis intensified my understanding of how conceptions of the PhD differ in relation to the macro frameworks of career cycle, PhD success or institutional role, before even considering the differences between subject areas or the individuality of personal interactions.

My major questions are educational ones: e.g. where does learning take place in the PhD, for both students and supervisors? A simple question, but one that is complicated to answer when recruitment of PGR (postgraduate research) students is on the increase at a time that funding councils and other non-university agencies are insisting on timely completion and improvement in graduate students' transferable skills. What makes the PhD risky is that the process is not as easily managed as some discourses imply. Rather it is a messy, stop-start process and problems occur in almost all PhDs – solving them is part of the educational process of becoming an independent researcher.

And the PhD is a difficult degree.

Many doctoral graduates will not enter academe, yet the PhD remains a key credential for an academic career and, as such, the demographics of who is successful in this degree becomes an equal opportunities' issue as it dictates the profile of future academe. As a point of entry it encompasses tacit knowledge about status rather than just professional achievement, and decisions about who is likely to show certain levels of academic achievement are still underpinned by social and cultural assumptions, however much the world has changed.

This book arose out of an individual National Teaching Fellowship (NTFS) award (for details of this scheme, see the Higher Education Academy website: www.heacademy.ac.uk/ourwork/professional/ntfs), which allowed me to carry out a project on PhD supervision. My intention was to deconstruct and reconstruct my thinking and my courses for supervisors and students. I use primary research data, which draws on accounts from people around the country: but the resulting collage is not a picture of any one university, department, faculty or student. Rather than providing a series of oversimplified hints and tips, it is an attempt to reflect the reality of supervision by acknowledging the huge variety in experience – of both supervisors and students – of all ages, nationalities and types of study. A lot of space is given to supervisors' accounts so that colleagues' experience can act as a resource to be drawn on. But also included are the views of successful students, current students, voices from those in non- academic, administrative and managerial roles in institutions as well as incorporating my own work as a trainer of supervisors and supporter of research students. The recognition underlying this approach is that individual viewpoints arise from experience that is, in turn, shaped by institutional context. This book does not write up a research project in the traditional sense, rather it reflects my journey in sifting information from a variety of sources, including my own experience. I spent a lot of time developing resources for my courses for supervisors; and working on, additionally, tutorials and innovative workshops for research students (such as supported writing weeks for research students).

At the time of my NTFS award, postgraduate research education and supervisor training had been taking up increasing amounts of my working life, without equivalent time to explore the background to all the changes that were happening. I have always been hugely impressed by the rationality of books and articles explaining how to supervise and how to be a successful student (and there are some excellent books). The notion that there are known ways of getting supervision right is intellectually attractive, but is a level of neatness I have never been able to introduce into my own supervision practice. Listening to the concerns and views of staff coming to supervisor training workshops that I provide, I have wanted to know more about how individual supervisors position themselves, how they function and accommodate pressure for change and how this sits against the powerful perspectives of research students' and colleagues' views. While this book does set supervision within its social context of multiple stakeholders who have legitimate concerns for standards, quality and outcomes of supervision, nonetheless I am primarily exploring the complexities of an educational experience, with the intention of developing courses that have relevance for participants.

I do acknowledge the sense of satisfaction, the joy in achievement and the benefits of intellectual growth that can come from both supervision and from the experience of studying for a PhD – not least because it is a major personal achievement to gain a PhD. But to achieve success requires acknowledgement of the inherently uncomfortable and difficult parts of the process. Two areas of clarity emerged from this project: that the perspective from which supervision is viewed produces distinctly different accounts of what supervision is (albeit containing 'family resemblances' across groups); and that the business of supervision and the PhD has to be understood as innately risky and challenging.

Outline of the book

Part 1: Setting the Scene: Chapters 1 and 2 address the complexity of supervisory roles and activities; and their positioning at the intersection of myriad pressures, both internal and external to the central relationship between supervisors and students and that emanate from inside and from outside universities.

- Chapter 1 considers supervision specifically as a form of teaching within the framework of recent pressures on higher education
- Chapter 2 draws from my own professional experience to outline the variety and complexity of the issues that can arise and need to be addressed during the PhD.

Part 2: Key Perspectives considers supervision and the experience of the PhD from a range of key perspectives:

- Chapter 3 presents views from past postgraduate research students who have successfully completed their PhDs
- Chapter 4 explores the experience of current students undergoing doctoral education
- Chapter 5 examines the perspective of a variety of university staff in administrative, support and management roles.

Part 3: Supervisors: old and new explores supervision from the perspective of supervisors:

- Chapter 6 provides an overview of issues from a range of supervisors
- Chapter 7 concerns new supervisors just setting out on their supervisory careers
- Chapter 8 draws on the understanding of experienced and successful supervisors.

Part 4 concludes with a discussion of supervisor training:

- Chapter 9 provides a discussion of supervisor training and development work and discusses key themes emerging from the whole book, with implications for students, supervisors and trainers.

A note on research

To help readers make sense of this book, I need to explain my view of the purposes of social research. I believe in gathering data and information of all kinds, and my reason for collecting data is a commitment to the idea that by understanding we can make changes – to actions, to institutions, to our professional practices, to society. Exploration, analysis and sifting of data have, for me, always been applied matters, holding within such scholarly actions the potential for change. I found an echo of my own feelings about research when reading McCormack's (2005) study of non-completers, in which one Master of Research student said:

> . . . I wanted to do things. I wanted not just to study it, but to do it . . . It would have been fine if I had just done another theoretical thesis, but to me that seemed a bit pointless . . . It just seemed like just another report that would get on a shelf and everyone would forget about it. (p. 240)

At heart, I am interested in the conversations held between individuals and their worlds: those interactions between what individuals bring with them to a situation in terms of cultural capital and what is constructed within the situation. These interactions – especially those that might be described as educational – are understood by me as containing affective as well as social and cognitive elements. The resulting phenomena being described within a social commentary which is accessible and which values social justice and inclusiveness.

A social commentary reflects awareness of the social context within which individuals make sense of their experience, which in the PhD is sometimes represented by disciplinary difference but goes far beyond these research communities – indeed the relevance of other vantage points is often eclipsed by the dominance of disciplinary difference in the debate. In this text, the lens through which I explore supervision is that of the macro framework within which individuals work: hence, I present data gathered from past as well as current students, experienced as well as new supervisors, and members of non-academic professions working within universities. These vantage points produce varied understandings of supervision and the PhD.

Like many essentially qualitative researchers (I say 'essentially' because I have always collected quantitative data too), I was originally inspired by grounded theory (Glaser and Strauss, 1967). This is no unswerving commitment to a method or approach from nearly 40 years ago (this would sound more like a religious faith than analytical questioning), and it is not automatic that every project I do can be described as sitting within a grounded-theory framework. But let me start with the elements of inspiration and consider how they related to this project.

First, Glaser and Strauss offered an example of how to work inductively within the kind of systematic, logical framework that typifies the development of research knowledge. Inductive approaches suit an iterative exploration concerned with moving beyond existing knowledge into new areas, un-nuanced and unquestioned areas, ones that are dominated by major theories or tacit assumptions that limit thinking. My preference is always for a comparative method of analysis in which data reflecting the research group's discussion of specific issues is compared. Looking for patterns and commonality, but also acknowledging the place of those who fall outside those patterns. Sifting data and looking for an account that has a ring of recognition to participants – yet hopefully presents their world back to them in a way that allows pause for thought and constructive reconsideration.

Yet I have never been a grounded theory purist, and my research reflects the times in which I have been a researcher. So the broad sweep of phenomenology and ethnology has influenced my research over many years: phenomenographic work has taken understanding of student learning to a new place since the 1970s, and anyone who now studies students' experience of learning must, inevitably, become a phenomenographer concerned with people's differing conceptions of phenomena (see Marton 1981, 1994). What is concerning, however, is phenomenography's potential to swallow up any research that explores educational experience via data reflecting the participants' perspectives, whatever the ontology or intent; whereas Cohen, Manion and Morrison (2007) describe *ethnography* as the broad strand of social research that 'needs to examine situations through the eyes of the participants' (p. 167). This project reflects the phenomenographic or ethnographic elements of tracing variations in human experience as viewed through their own perspectives. However, my aim was to produce action, not hard and fast categories; I wanted to view supervision through the lens of multiple perspectives in order to open out understanding of supervision and the PhD, and what I then did as a practitioner.

Hence, the approach underlying this project has much in common with action research, not least in the expectation that research should ultimately impact on social practice and bring about change; and in the narrow goal of developing courses as an outcome of data collection. Cohen *et al.* have expertly summarized the reflexive, cyclical and politically emancipatory nature of action research (pp. 297–313), plus its relaxed acceptance of what constitutes data, describing it as 'a flexible, situationally responsive methodology that offers rigour, authenticity and voice' (p. 312). However, the importance placed on collaborative work in action research is not evident in this project, except in those elements little described here: the development of appropriate curricula (for research students and for supervisors) which have been worked through jointly with colleagues both informally and formally (e.g. in extensive public discussion via committees and accrediting bodies and through the responses of past course members).

As well as being a researcher conducting interviews and using questionnaires, I could also be described as a participant-observer: I have been a research student; I have been a supervisor (successfully and unsuccessfully, according to current criteria); I have examined research degrees and have, myself, been examined at doctoral level; and I have both provided development courses for supervisors and externally examined other people's supervisor modules. At the time of writing I have worked for over 20 years with a steady succession of PhD students who have run into difficulties with their degrees. The outcomes of my analysis, then, must bear elements of auto-ethnography and high levels of reflection: reflection on teaching is a key tool for anyone involved in one-to-one tutorial work, and almost as an extension of this habit, what action researchers would call reflexiveness (see Cohen *et al.*, p. 310) – the self-conscious awareness of myself in the research. This is a contentious use of the word 'reflexive' in the world of qualitative researchers: Silverman (2005) has written that reflexivity is 'mistakenly used to refer to self-questioning by a researcher' and, rather, means 'the self-organizing character of all interaction so that any action provides for its own context' (p. 379). But, in line with the simpler definition of reflexivity, one of my goals was to develop further my courses for supervisors, so unpicking and reconstructing my own knowledge had to be a part of the project.

I am, of course, assuming that epistemology can encompass the subjective accounts, of both researchers and researched. Analysis both reflects that subjectivity and moves beyond it in a process of integration. What becomes available to the reader is a mirror to hold up to their own experience and measure it against these accounts – and, in so doing, see reflected something that is perhaps known but seen again in a new light. In these ways, practice and practitioner knowledge moves forward. System in collecting, sifting accounts and testing them with other groups is a part of constructing an authentic analysis, even though the outcome cannot reflect each reader's experience. Constructing a commentary in this style, does, of course, imply the expectation of a limited form of generalizability (perhaps what Williams, 2002, has called '*moderatum* generalizations') – at least in the expectation that my account should contain familiar, transferable elements. My commentary is the result of a personal journey, where anonymous accounts are woven together with my teaching experience and scholarship, resulting in elements of 'factitious' or 'fictive' description. Rather than implying 'imagined', however, these terms denote that descriptions belong to no person or place, but represent regular (sometimes frequent, sometimes less frequent) events and experiences.

Collecting data in waves forced me to confront the ways that difficult problems occur in all supervision, and that what distinguishes better and worse supervision is how supervisors and students manage problems. Whereas a style of research that (a) reads the literature (b) sets up research questions and (c) collects data to answer those questions would have left me in danger of embedding my original, easy dichotomies into the core of a project on this subject. Collecting, analysing and sifting data in waves allows questions to be changed, let me build on previous knowledge and test out emerging understandings with further groups and individuals – and to sift out where the data is presenting a picture different to the ideas one started out with. The research phases (with numbers of participants in brackets) were:

Phase 1: Exploration

- exploratory questionnaires with supervisors (15)
- exploratory questionnaires for new supervisors attending supervision courses (20)
- exploratory questionnaires for successfully completed PhD students (19).

Phase 2: Interviews

- interviews with supervisor-managers and/or administrators (8)
- interviews with new supervisors (8)
- interviews with experienced supervisors (12).

Phase 3: Surveys

- questionnaires returned to me by supervisors (108)
- questionnaires from current PGR students (114).

The existing literature has a complex place within this framework. For by reading the literature first, there is a danger of setting up researcher questions based on the agendas of other writers, rather than truly sifting data in an iterative style. Yet research cannot happen in isolation, good scholarship requires the enrichment of work already achieved not just as a basis on which to build, but also as a sounding board and with which to disagree. In a sense, the existing literature works, in traditional grounded style, as another source of data to be sifted as a route to understanding current concerns and solutions. I have taken the route in this book of linking literature to the key themes emerging from the data collected, as a tool to help analyse and explain patterns emerging. In this sense, existing literature is seen as living in an interactive relationship with data – rather than as a separate process designed to position the research and the researcher.

The process of producing an informed social commentary (which I view as another version of what Glaser and Strauss meant by 'middle level theory', or the critical theory of action theorists) is inherent in the journey of collecting and engaging with data, but includes the researcher as a real actor rather than a narrator pretending to be standing to one side of events. Social commentary must always be quasi-historical and contextualized socially, allowing for discussion of change and development as societies negotiate tensions around key activities, yet the ethnographic element of participant-observation requires the researcher's presence. Dawn Johnston and Tom Strong (2008) use a 'voicing metaphor' to describe the student Dawn's process of making meaning and finding 'one's own academic and personal voice' (abstract):

> Each voice Dawn consulted as she wrote had his or her own ideas and purposes, often with an authority accorded them by others ... out of this polyphony of voices (think of a cacophonous marching band of voices instead of musical instruments, all metaphorically marching to different drummers) was a 'heteroglossic' challenge of creating meaning that fit her purpose and those of the academic exercise. (p. 48)

While I remain hesitant about claiming the self-revelatory centrality of the autoethnographer, nonetheless this exposition of the presence of the researcher is one that describes well what I mean.

I have selected the route of using interviews and questionnaires to limit the invasion of people's lives. Throughout my research, participants had opportunity to opt out and I kept to forms of research that leave participants control over the extent to which they contributed. Anonymity and confidentiality, for me, go well beyond concealing names and details (such as occupations), and must hold good in 20 years' time when individuals have changed their viewpoints. So, for example, in analysis I use limited amounts of the extensive material gathered to illustrate themes emerging rather than presenting recognizable case studies. I construct 'fictive' (or 'factive') cases from a variety of sources of data, so that the result is no person or situation in particular. The formal stages of information-gathering started in 2004, plus I draw on my prior experience over two decades of teaching research students and, more recently, supervisors. Hence, this is not an account of particular people at any particular time or place, rather a picture woven from numerous strands collected in the UK over long periods of time.

The resulting account is, in part, a form of fiction but one that is based on the careful sifting of primary data. In all my examples, people, departments and universities are not recognizable: I use 'factional/fictive' scenarios (or vignettes) to represent situations I meet regularly and some are merged – and so they represent no one individual or event. Gender, ages, nationalities have been changed where not changing them might make situations, places or people appear recognizable.

Analysing and interpreting supervision

This project occurred within the context of a recent explosion in publications on the subject of PhD supervision, especially in Australian writing, that attempts to theorize this diverse activity. There is a tension between approaches, reflected in what might be called the apprenticeship (personalized) and administrative (processual) analyses of doctoral supervision, although I maintain that these two perspectives are not sufficient of themselves to make sense of the developmental, risky elements in what is primarily an educational enterprise.

In the apprenticeship model, research students are viewed as undergoing an apprenticeship, not just in the sense that they may become academics, but because they are indentured to a master who ensures entry to the research guild. Supervision is not teaching in the obvious sense of providing lectures, curricula and related assessments (except on some doctoral programmes). Rather, supervision arises out of a supervisor's research persona and its associated discourse of academic autonomy and membership of international research communities. The notion of apprenticeship has been under pressure from governments and funders in the last decade (see Chapter 1 for further discussion of this), plus the range of newly available styles of PhD programme have undermined supervision as a relatively private matter between one supervisor and one student (Park, 2005). Traditionally, becoming indentured requires one master and so it is a model that struggles to encompass joint or team supervision.

The recent prevalence of what might be called an 'administrative analysis' is not about administrators' involvement in the PhD, but one which focuses on managing the PhD systematically as a series of monitored stages intended to lead to the completion of theses. Acknowledgement of an administrative analysis means recognition that there are numerous additional stakeholders besides supervisors with an interest in what happens to PhD students: governments around the world who fund students, the UK government which has taken a closer interest in the useful outcomes of education, funding bodies, central administrators and those who provide support – other students, their families, and university managers. Park (2007) acknowledges the influence of limited employment opportunities within universities on students' motivations to study PhDs, and the resulting expectation that money that backs research training will produce graduates with transferable skills relevant to a wide range of employers (p. 17).

The administrative model reflects how the recent history of the PhD has been about change, and much of that change can be understood as attempts to manage and minimise risk. An administrative model does not, however, fully answer how a supervisor manages risk while allowing space for students to grow and develop within the current policy context. So, for example, while not necessarily becoming professional academics themselves, graduate researchers must negotiate the standards maintained by disciplinary gatekeepers while working at the edges of that discipline's research problems. Morley *et al.* (2002) argue that study guides allow the assumption that doctoral education is known and understood, requiring only clear explanation to students, a viewpoint with which they take issue by using Bourdieu and Passeron's concepts of 'habitus' and 'artistry':

> While these study guides may be useful, they fail to take into account the subterranean agendas of values and ideologies in doctoral assessment. Hence, a thesis might conform to the technicalities of a quality product, but can fail the assessment as a result of a clash of belief systems. The emphasis on technicist preparations is not just an oversimplification, but a misunderstanding of the process of acquiring habitus and artistry, as well as sponsorships and networks, in this as in any other professional training. . . . (p. 268)

In taking us to the relational aspects of 'becoming' (a researcher, an academic, a successful PhD student, and academic writer), Morley *et al.* are clear about the power relations in the work of gatekeeping. While by no means suggesting that all aspects of supervision and examining are based on unfairness, they are explicit in their view that current structures foster the potential for and retention of irrational and unfair elements. Hence, a processual, administrative model offers opportunities for optimism and rationality, but overlooks the riskiness of PhD reality.

Where Morley *et al.* take issue with study guides, Grant (2001) argues against institutional codes of practice for doctoral education (or, at least, the *University of Auckland: Supervision of Theses and Dissertations at Master's Level*), specifically for their lack of recognition of 'the place and play of power, desire, and difference in supervision' (p. 16). Calling these 'clean codes', Grant argues that by not recognizing what she calls 'dirt' (described as 'cultural matter out of place', p. 13), such codes do not work in terms of quality assurance and may be dangerous 'because it legitimates an unrealistic picture of supervision as a fundamentally reasonable practice' (p. 23). Hence, the ability to complete a thesis is assumed in an administrative model (successful outcome is written into a successful system) – but this is not necessarily assumed by supervisors or by students. Yet from outside universities, it can be hard to see why those selected with good qualifications cannot make the doctoral grade (indeed, hard, also, to fathom how 1980s social science supervisors could justify getting less than a quarter through to timely graduation, as is discussed in Chapter 1).

While the concerns of the apprenticeship and administrative models should be of importance to all interested in supervision and both inform my analysis, what is emphasized here is an educational dimension to the discussion of the PhD: one in which intellectual development is of central concern (including, of course, successful completion). In this model, the relational aspects of the degree – between staff and students, staff-students and subject matter, between supervisors, students and their disciplinary context, and their various expectations and assumptions and approaches to supervision as a form of teaching – take centre-stage in relation to educational development. Understanding of supervision and the PhD are further contextualized within institutional and professional perspectives.

Important in this educational model is the place of risk and riskiness, in both process and outcomes. HEFCE (2005) have referred to risk for part-time students in registering for a PhD; however, their concern is with the risks being high that students will not complete their PhD in a timely fashion (p. 3, and p. 32, para. 107). Rather than being a matter of occasional relevance, the risks of change (or not changing), developing (or not) and learning at this profound, developmental level, become central to understanding the educational process PhD students undergo. So this approach constructs supervision as a form of developmental teaching, albeit often carried out by active researchers whose primary commitment is to one or more international academic reference groups.

It is a subject about which many cared passionately and I am grateful to all who contributed for their detailed and considered responses to my questions. Thanks too, to my colleagues for smoothing my path: Tim Ellis (for help with online questionnaires); Brian Francis (for statistical advice); and Chris Park; members of the Centre for the Enhancement for Learning and Teaching, especially Ali Cooper, Louise Innes, Tony Luxon and Kerry Swindlehurst. Particular thanks for (variously) patience and wise words to Brian Francis, Rosemary Peelo and Keith Soothill.

What follows is a series of pictures of the PhD and supervision, constructed over a long period of time and informed by research, scholarship, teaching and working in universities. These pictures were drawn together during a project whose main aim was to inform and develop my teaching of supervisors and research students. While this is not an account of any individual supervisors, students or universities, I hope it is recognizable to anyone who follows those paths and that it might contribute to understanding the PhD and the work of supervision.

Part 1
Setting the Scene

Chapters 1 and 2 address the complexity of supervisory roles and activities; and their positioning at the intersection of myriad pressures, both internal and external to the central relationship between supervisors and students and that emanate from inside and from outside universities. Part 1 explores some of the ways in which supervision can be described as 'teaching'. It discusses what constitutes 'risk' for students and supervisors and how the social and cultural structures of research education and universities impact on the experiences of supervisors and students.

Teaching, Learning and Taking Risks

1

Chapter Outline

'Supervision' covers a complex range of tasks that require supervisors to take developmental approaches to teaching as well as to exercise a variety of high-level social and research skills. This chapter explores some of the risks and tensions arising out of external pressures as well as arising from within supervisory relationships and disciplines. It considers supervision as a form of teaching: exploring the teaching of writing as an example of how doctoral students are learning social practices as well as academic skills; and considers risk in relation to subject specialism, including some of the ways in which students might experience risk.

Supervision is an umbrella term, indicating a broad range of activity but not providing any sense of its detailed demands. In part, this stems from the variety that constitutes doctoral work: not only do disciplines and subjects vary hugely in their views of what constitutes a PhD, but there is also variety in the doctorates themselves, including those studied on doctoral programmes, in the workplace, presented for examination via publication, or those pursued in the traditional mode of research project and thesis production.

In this study, the PhD was taken to refer to research education and innovative advancement in a discipline or subject area (rather than a generic higher degree beyond Master's level as described, for example, by Doncaster and

Lester, 2002); and yet the PhD and, hence, the doctoral experience of supervision, is not a homogeneous educational process. There is, though, a common theme: one that sees students set out on a journey of research, a process of learning and 'becoming' a scholar and skilled researcher and innovator in their field, and anticipate becoming accredited as such. These journeys are risky and focus on forms of learning that require guides, mentors and, on occasions, instructors.

The role of 'teacher' is contested in higher education: although teaching is central to the lives of most academics, neither professional identities nor teaching styles can be fully gleaned from this. When it comes to the place of supervision in academic identities, life can become even more complicated. As we will see in Chapter 2, the place of research in academe is deemed by some to have changed and to have become more privileged; and there are regular debates about the possibility of splitting teaching from research. There can be a hierarchical element to this: if research is seen as more important than teaching and supervision is the outcome of success in one's research identity, then there can be resistance to seeing supervision as a form of teaching. I have been on the receiving end of colleagues' feelings (ranging from irritation and rudeness through to annoyance and anger) during supervisor courses on this subject – *'I am* not *a teacher'*; *'supervision is not a relationship, it's about research'*; *'good students don't need teaching'*.

Even for those who accept supervision as a teaching role, it is a complex form of teaching. Not least, the picture of doctoral work as following straight on from an undergraduate or Master's degree, funded and enrolled full time in a university in which students are resident is, to an extent, out of tune with life. Students may be part time, and studying at a distance, perhaps visiting their university only occasionally. Some may be colleagues, working within the institution at which they study or at neighbouring universities. Students fund their studies in a variety of ways, with backing from one of the famous funding bodies being open only to a limited percentage of doctoral students. Many students' expectations of how they will be treated must, in part, be framed by understanding themselves if not as paying customers then as clients paying premium rates for professional services. Leonard *et al.* (2004) describe how the Institute of Education's doctoral students are frequently engaged in vocational advancement in already established careers and well-embedded in the world of work, already highly experienced and unlikely to switch careers to become academics. Far removed from a traditional picture of research students, their diversity illustrates how the needs of research council-funded students (which has driven the recent supervision agenda) appears to relate only tangentially to many doctoral students.

Further, supervision has moved from a taken-for-granted activity to one that is much questioned, occurring as it does in a context of recent and rapid change – change that is commonly described as driven by the insistence of funders and governments that doctoral education is opened up to public scrutiny and an underlying belief that universities have not been performing well in this regard (see, for example, Park, 2007 on drivers for change, pp. 13–24). As a result, successful supervision in the UK is now often assumed to be synonymous with successful completion within four years; and, ergo, non-completion has become synonymous with poor supervision.

Has there been past justification for this view that supervisors and universities were failing to deliver? Rudd's seminal book (1985) contains a synopsis of studies concerning completion, which give some insight into the funding bodies' decisions to become more vigilant in monitoring how their money was used. Completion rates are difficult to estimate, but Rudd reported how the establishment of the Swinnerton-Dyer Working Party on Postgraduate Education (which reported in 1982) spurred funding councils into compiling figures, resulting in some shocking findings. The now classic division in completion rates between sciences and social sciences was made clear: 47.8 per cent of Science and Engineering Research Council (SERC)-funded doctoral students who started in October 1979 had submitted a thesis by October 1983; this was in comparison with 24.9 per cent of Social Science Research Council students (these would now be ESRC students, p. 10). Rudd commented that science and technology students '. . .gain their doctorates more quickly. . .' and '. . .are more likely to be more successful eventually. . .' than arts and social science students (p. 11). The figures for social science students hid further differences, not least according to the numbers of grants received, as ESRC figures showed:

> Those getting the larger numbers of awards accounted for 72 per cent of the total going to the universities and a completion rate of 24.5 per cent, compared with 18.9 per cent for those institutions having fewer. (p.11)

Nonetheless, those institutions getting the lion's share of grants could hardly be said to have been performing well.

As a result, the ESRC stopped awarding grants for students to study in departments with poor submission rates. The subsequent rise in numbers of completions among grant-holding students perhaps confirmed the suspicion that, left to their own devices, universities will not deliver in this area of work and require strong management. So, for example, McClellan (2005) reported on the efficacy of funding bodies' 'zero-tolerance approach' to poor completion rates (which can now include the blacklisting of whole institutions), with the ESRC having seen 'the proportion of PhDs completed within four years jump from 29 per cent in 1981 to 84 per cent in 1999'.

More recent concerns from outside universities about PhD supervision have added other layers of concern beyond those of the mid-1980s of successful and timely completion:

> The key drivers of change are a growing emphasis on skills and training, on submission and completion rates, and on quality of supervision, along with changes in the examination of the thesis, and the introduction of benchmarking. (Park, 2005, p. 192)

While the criteria for successful supervision may have become more easily codified (e.g. timely completion and development of transferable skills), supervision itself has remained a complex activity in which clarity about its goals does not necessarily show what makes these outcomes attainable.

Not all are convinced, in addition, that such clarity of focus is sufficient at doctoral level and question whether the goals of innovation and originality are achieved via monitoring and training programmes alone. Whitelock *et al.* (2008) argue that academic and research rigour should be matched with academic playfulness, seeing supervision as an arena for supporting student risk taking through the 'exploration of ideas and possible avenues of research' (p. 148). This notion of doctoral education implies a level of creativity in the enterprise; Park (2005) has described research students as the 'stewards of a discipline' in that they keep it alive and 'intellectually vibrant' through innovation in thought, knowledge and in conceptualization of a subject (p. 191). The doubt for some supervisors lies in whether such innovation can happen in tight timeframes and to order.

Bendix Petersen (2007) argues for understanding the socializing nature of the PhD and that, regardless of future careers, students are learning 'academicity' not necessarily as a future role but as an identity; and the supervisory relationship is a key place for negotiating what is academic and what is 'other':

> Something about their acts and articulations places them outside of the boundary separating the academic from the non-academic, Other. (p. 478)

Hence, students making bids to become acceptable within a 'particular discourse community' cannot 'perform contextually unintelligible or inappropriate academicity' (p. 478). Delamont *et al.* (1997) explored the ways in which research groups in the natural sciences provide the locus for constructing pedagogic continuity within a subject area; and, rather than *critical mass* as the key component in the doctoral process (the principle for focusing resources recommended in the 1996 Harris Report), they argue for an understanding of the group process as part of socializing students in becoming scientists. This process, they argue, is resistant to being replicated in other subject areas, given the intricate entwining of academic *habitus* and subject knowledge. A supervisor, then, can be seen as a gatekeeper for particular academic communities, whatever the career goals of the student.

Supervision as teaching

One of the prime difficulties in making sense of supervisory teaching is the sheer range of skills and activities expected of supervisors, as Bartlett and Mercer (2001) have described:

> The impromptu list we devised looked a bit like this: confidante, source of intellectual inspiration, resource manager, grant application writer, navigator of institutional tangles, manager of change, personal motivator, writing teacher, editor, career mentor, and networker – and those were just some of the most readily identified roles. Given the broad parameters of the relationship then, it's not surprising that the field is littered with grim tales of disappointing supervision experiences. (p. 4)

I would add 'subject area gatekeeper' and 'international' to Bartlett and Mercer's lists of skills and contextual factors, placing membership of internationalized research community as more central to many supervisors' academic, research identities than the role of teacher.

Hockey (1996) gets round the issue of whether supervisors wish to be seen as teachers or not by drawing on Rapoport *et al.*'s (1989) model of tutorship: Hockey presents a notion of tutorship which is informal, comradely and professional. It is, perhaps, the expectation of an informal and comradely relationship in particular which explains his finding that supervisors varied in their ability to recognize the trouble that students were in and that for those

> . . . with limited experience of this kind, the speed of acknowledgement tended to be slower, with the result that the problem of research impetus had more time to develop. (p. 362)

The nature of the supervisory teaching–learning relationship is then, para-doxically, a part of what gets in the way of making difficult judgements about progression – and that difficult judgements, perhaps unsurprisingly, become more manageable the greater experience one has of them.

Wisker *et al.* (2003) offer a 'dialogues' framework describing student–supervisor interactions. In style, these echo Whitelock *et al.*'s quest for creativ-ity in supervision; and they are modelled as strategies to help students develop autonomy and take responsibility for their work. Variations in dia-logue are described according to students' stage in progression – 'proposals, progress reports and the completed/nearly completed PhD' (p. 391). Pole and Sprokkereef (1997) illustrate how, in their study of supervisors in physics, mathematics and engineering, a complex range of activities is required differ-entially at different points in the students' progress, commenting:

> The list of tasks can be endless and will vary in relation to the different needs of students at different times in their PhD careers and to the demands of the discipline in which the doctorate is being pursued. (p. 50)

Part of exercising these high-level skills includes working with adults in a collegial way, even when students' development may not occur according to a pre-set timetable – requiring fine judgements concerning when to leave people to develop or when to ring alarm bells. Because there are no obviously rights answers in such dilemmas, these judgements are inherently risky.

While borrowing a notion of 'tutorial' relationship as the basic building block of supervisory teaching, nonetheless one must recognize that this relationship is mediated through subject matter – indeed, it is the lack of this mediation that limits an administrative analysis of doctoral education (one that looks primarily at the overall process, stages and outcomes). It is com-monplace to argue that PhD supervision cannot be understood outside disci-plines because each one is different: I would argue that this is too weak a description of the socializing process at work, for, rather, *all* PhDs share the primacy of subject matter in shaping the experience, and hence teaching and learning take place within a triangle of students-supervisors-subject matter. Delamont *et al.* have described the ways in which the 'research group' tradition in natural sciences is a means by which knowledge is reproduced; and this group relationship with knowledge construction shapes, in turn, the supervi-sory style as one which sets the overall frame and research direction, problems to be solved, funding and resourcing, while day-to-day supervision is carried out by postdoctoral researchers. This is quite different to the humanities' tradition of one supervisor accepting a research focus chosen by the student. Supervisory teaching is, then, understood as a contextualized activity and developmental in nature – taking place within a specific and public arena, that of a disciplinary discourse.

The natural science 'group model' of supervision illustrates how supervision may not appear as teaching in traditional ways: it is less about telling a student what they need to know (although this may happen occasionally) but more about encouraging situations, writing and discussions which enable students to deepen their capacity to conceptualize and communicate their analysis. High levels of communicative competence are needed on the part of both supervisors and students to negotiate this sort of developmental teaching. While this is a social interchange, with all the required sophistication of reading another human being, it is also about intellectual change and challenge. Hence, supervisors are often in the position of critic: it is a rare and deft supervisor who can regularly challenge students yet encourage confidence and growth at the same time. The likelihood of both parties reading from the same page at the same time are limited.

Developing academic skills and social practices: the example of writing

While, on occasions, a supervisor may be teaching specific skills (such as postdocs instructing on the use of particular lab equipment or a method for solving a mathematical problem), problems arise when the *developmental* implications of the skills' element are overlooked. Developing as a writer is one example of how a simplistic, task-based approach is not always sufficient to ensure progress. When asked to provide writing courses, for example, I have found that what people mean by 'writing' is not always clear: do they mean, for example, editing, drafting, planning, rhetoric or exploratory writing? It is often assumed that how one writes is known, and students just need to be given clear instructions. Experience has taught me that different disciplinary groups write, question and research in different ways and that these go beyond stylistic techniques to more fundamental epistemological beliefs. This experience has, over time, brought me closer in understanding to what is now described as an 'academic literacies' tradition (see, for example, Crème and Lea, 2003), via Swales' (1990) more static work on genres. Nonetheless, I am aware of dangers in analysing the writing of specific genres of overlooking the fast-changing and varied elements possible within dynamic subject areas.

In addition to disciplinary differences, students vary in how they approach reading, writing and research. Torrance and Thomas's (1994) study, while allowing for general, cross-disciplinary writing courses, nonetheless acknowledge differences between individual students in their approaches to writing. Not least, by distinguishing between 'knowledge-telling' and 'knowledge-transforming' approaches they allow the complexity of the writing task to be recognized. 'Knowledge telling', they argue, is closely related to the naïve 'think-then-write' approaches currently commonplace in writing advice; whereas 'knowledge-transforming' allows for revision of text to lead to changes in content as part of knowledge construction. This latter approach begins to take us far away from the notion that writing is solely a technical skill that can be explained in occasional hour-long classes, to a model of writing as part of a process of constructing ideas and knowledge and hence integral to research itself.

In Torrance and Thomas's study, some students managed well with planning, but many did not. Those who mixed planning with transformative strategies appeared most worried by the thesis writing task, where those with either clear planning or clear transformative approaches were less worried. They concluded: '. . . it may be important to alert students who are unsuccessful when using the think-and-write approach to knowledge-transforming approaches' (p. 113). This advice runs counter to practices I have encountered frequently, where attempts to manage the messiness of PhD students' progress are made by insisting that they produce a detailed thesis outline at an early stage in proceedings.

My own view has long been that to enable students to learn, either performable skills or in a wider, developmental way, one must understand the social context and individual affective elements as well as cognitive aspects of learning (Peelo 1994, 2002) – the individual student's conversation with their world, both personal and academic. Students' concern about appropriate writing style (picked out by Torrance and Thomas as one potential area of worry) is more than a technical choice. Tone, language construction and vocabulary all reflect understanding of an international epistemological discourse (and one developed across generations) alongside organization of material and of argument (often called 'discipline' as a shorthand); and in so doing, reflect student attempts to position themselves and their work within chosen communities – establishing a public, academic identity. Hence, anxiety around writing can, in part, be interpreted as performance anxiety even if the task itself is carried out relatively privately.

Such tension between writing technique and forming an intellectual identity echoes Bendix Petersen's thesis of doctoral education as a time of negotiating academicity and is a theme taken up in Kamler and Thomson's (2004) work on writing abstracts. Here they lay out their view that postgraduate writing is a part of qualitative research and, rather than taking a surface, textual approach to developing writing skills they recognize writing as a social practice. So, their concern with writing abstracts is a part of their wider interest in how 'students learn to write and become authorised writers within particular scholarly and institutional communities . . .' (pp. 196–7). Abstracts, in this framework, are considered as '. . . both text work and identity work . . . as a bid for finding an authoritative speaking position, and asserting what one knows in a field of expert and interested others' (p. 197). Most specifically, they suggest that struggling to write abstracts may be related to postgraduates' novice position hence 'may have less to do with writing competence than with being accomplished in taking up a deferential academic speaking position' (p. 197). Unsurprisingly then, they stress that they are not talking about skills but writing practices, and that '. . . advice and tip will not suffice . . .' (p. 207).

The PhD, then, is difficult to define because of the variety of academic practices and contexts in which it takes place and, hence, the range of activities, abilities and skills required of supervisors across the long period of students' registration do not lend themselves to easy systematization. Nonetheless, the supervisory relationship can be typified: as a form of educational interaction focusing on research; including (or with an expectation of) a style of tutoring or developmental teaching that is closer and more personal than other forms of teaching; taking place over a longer period of time than most other teaching; and rooted in both the student and supervisor's relationships with a disciplinary community. Where, then, are the elements of riskiness if supervision can be so easily summarized?

Subject specialism and risk

In broad terms, science PhDs appeared as less problematic in Rudd's findings and this reputation has persisted. Science students are often assumed to have a clear focus for research, perhaps working in teams and labs with their work a part of a larger project, and researching with known methods. While Delamont *et al.* (1997) have illustrated the centrality of pedagogic continuity in some natural science subjects, nonetheless over half the SERC-funded doctoral students who started in October 1979 had not finished four years later: so, even in areas seen as more successful, teams can go wrong, equipment may not work and money runs out. In contrast to the 'team model' version of science, arts and social science PhDs appear idiosyncratic, and given the current fashion for meta-theorization and innovation in research methods, what external examiners may decide in a viva can seem mysterious. As Delamont *et al.* argue:

> Epistemological and methodological wrangling, and contested theoretical 'positions' are characteristic of the social sciences and the humanities . . . [which] are more likely to aspire to 'rebellious' scholarship, conducted in a more loosely framed social and intellectual context. (p. 548)

But more specific than these broad-brush generalizations, Bendix Petersen (2007) reminds us that subject-specialism is an essential ingredient in supervisors' academic identities, and an important part of students' nascent intellectual and (sometimes) work identities. Yet subject matter is also part of what makes a PhD a risky enterprise. Park, as we have seen, has summarized the importance of research students in sustaining the intellectual vibrancy of disciplines. Risk, then, is new subject matter, on the edge, taking understanding forward and on sufficient scale to be worthwhile and to be carried out over a long time period (three to four years). This allows for three immediate potential pitfalls: that the project may not sufficiently address what is, by definition, a difficult problem; that the scale of research turns out to be too complicated, not sufficient or not manageable; and that such problems can be dealt with, but not within the timeframe (of universities, of funding, of how much of their life a student can dedicate to this activity).

There is no supervisory relationship without subject matter: but there are at least two sets of understandings, expectations and conceptualizations of the subject matter within a supervisory relationship (or relationships, given the advent of joint and panel supervision), hence the personal and the professional become intertwined. Paradigm clashes and profound differences of opinion between student and supervisor can complicate a PhD. In a world of supervisory teams, one supervisor may have relevant experience but be rooted in an entirely different perspective, a situation in which compromise is not always an option. There is, additionally, the (often) unspoken risk that the student may not make the transition from promising recruit to independent researcher. They may struggle with any element of planning and execution of the actual research, before considering matters such as writing and argumentation. For many, especially social science and humanities students, the level of conceptualization needed may not happen sufficiently in the time available, to avoid the process being especially painful.

Rudd's suggestion was that many problems would be solved if students were not funded for a PhD until they had worked through a literature review and a detailed proposal first (p. 118), and this solution is currently mirrored in a student's prior Master's study and the uses made of Year One in PhD studies. However, whatever administrative systems are set in place, it must be said that the nature of research is to be risky: new areas, of necessity, should provide researchers with problems to solve (whether these are conceptual, matters of experimentation and equipment, access to data or access to specific populations). Had these problems already been solved, then there would be no 'unknown', no level of difficulty with which to engage.

PhD experience and risk

Students travel round the world, give up jobs, dislocate families, struggle for funds – all for a degree in which there can be no more guarantees about success than undergraduates registering for a first degree might expect. For students who register as full time and who are resident at the university of their choice, there can be a sense of dislocation and isolation, for even those who have studied at their chosen university in the UK before are viewing their institution from a new vantage-point. Students start a new working relationship with supervisors, for which only few have experienced anything similar, and begin a project that while once exciting inevitably runs into periods of dreariness and toil. Part-time students may be juggling work and families with research, and often at a distance from the institution. So few of the (apparent) benefits of being in a research community are available to them and there will be fewer opportunities to get to understand new supervisors on an informal basis.

All of these elements are uncomfortable to some extent, and people manage them differently according to the structures of their lives and personal histories. But with the PhD, no matter what one's previous academic success, there is no real way of telling who is going to manage to succeed and who is not. Intellectual development is not a straightforward process because it has a transformational element, hence people do not perform to timetable. *Tasks* may be ticked off a list at regular intervals – but the more understanding of complex research methods, theorization and conceptualization is required, the less one can predict which students are going to make it through to the end. Data sets do not arrive without problems: experiments may not succeed, access to research populations may not happen. Along the way, a potentially successful student needs to metamorphose into an independent researcher, a professional writer, teacher and communicator.

Most PhDs students will face challenges of some sort – they will lose track of what they are doing, where they are going and what the thesis is about. They will change their minds about the place of academe in their identity and in their futures. Crises will occur, indeed, one might argue that they *must* occur to move the project forward. Finding ways through these difficulties contributes to the joy and sense of achievement at getting a PhD.

Certainly, in my support role I am unable to tell who will get the PhD. I have seen the most sensitive, nervous, edgy people come from far, far behind and get through vivas with flying colours; while others who appear to have moved steadily and smoothly cannot bring themselves to write up and be examined. Apparent plodders come through, in the end, with clear and sparkling analyses of interest and originality, while others who started off as high fliers become stolid and stodgy in their conceptualization. Not being able to predict in every case who will succeed means, to me, that each supervisor walks into a risky situation each time they agree to take on a student – no promises can be made realistically on either side.

Likewise, the student takes a risk. Supervisors may be excellent in all sorts of ways: they may be personable, welcoming and expert in a relevant academic field. However, they may not yet have examined many theses and have supervised only a few other students. Hence, their nerve and expertise when things go wrong may not be the strongest. Perhaps they are experts in the subject, highly experienced examiners and supervisors; yet they may be lacking human sensitivity and, over years of supervising, have lost their excitement and interest in the face of yet another student stumbling through the mists of a PhD. Perhaps they no longer have the patience to allow a student to develop their own thesis, dealing with time limits and administrative procedures by insisting on a particular thesis shape and nature of analysis. Others may never have had the necessary personal style, no matter how successful as researchers: Freedman (2003) describes with unusual directness how the supervision style of the formidable economist George Stigler was not conducive to dissertation supervision, however great the academic, commenting:

> Good, even great, economists do not necessarily make successful teachers at that level. In contrast, graduate work and particularly locating an appropriate supervisor is more like a search for a congenial marriage partner. (p. 287)

The risks in matching up are great – realistically, the odds on a match being absolutely right are long.

When the PhD feels difficult, students may lose faith as they recognize the ways in which their supervisors are less capable than they originally imagined. Hockey (1996) reported on a study of supervisors and explored the phenomenon of student–supervisor relations when students' motivation and momentum was in doubt. Supervisors, he argued, can lose belief in their students: he described how, in his empirical study of supervisors, a breakdown of trust could be discerned on the part of supervisors:

> Some supervisor/student relationships were characterised by a breakdown of trust on the part of supervisors, who came to doubt whether the student possessed the required energy, intellectual acumen and motivation to carry out the agreed programme of work, despite oral warnings. (p. 364)

While there are a range of problems a student may face, those of 'momentum' particularly challenge supervisors, hence Hockey was exploring whether or not student–supervisor contracts could be useful where the relationship had run into motivational trouble. Successful negotiation of a period of loss of trust will depend on excellent social and communication skills on both sides, and may well be typified by miscommunication, misunderstanding and frustration on the part of both supervisor and student.

It was clear in Hockey's study (as it is in this one) that supervisors did not see intelligence and prior qualifications as sufficient for PhD success; rather, that it requires a collection of personal characteristics. Drawing on other studies, Hockey establishes a consensus concerning those qualities that supervisors associated with a 'good' student: 'such students are expected to display intelligence, independence, initiative, enthusiasm, creativity, perseverance and willingness to consider supervisory advice' (pp. 360–1). Some of these characteristics were borrowed for questionnaires in this study, combined with others that emerged from my exploratory work with both staff and students, and were recognized by both groups as key ingredients for success (see chapters 4 and 6 particularly). By inference, in Hockey's study a 'difficult' student was not necessarily one who runs into problems, so much as one who does not respond to the supervisor's interventions:

> . . . supervisors revealed that in other instances neither encouragement nor warnings were to any avail, the thesis did not progress, and even more problematic episodes ensued, with the actual supervisory relationship itself becoming increasingly fraught. (p. 362)

Recognition of what are often defined as motivational problems may also be linked with the challenge supervisors face in finding the balance between students' freedom to develop, and the level of monitoring needed in each individual case. Student problem-solving is part of the PGR agenda, and not everyone develops at the same rate or in the same way. How, then, do supervisors allow learning to take place and also know when developmental challenges have not been met but have, instead, metamorphosed into motivational problems? The expectation of egalitarianism in mentoring and tutoring students (not exactly the same as equality of power between student and supervisor) places supervisors in difficulty when the thesis begins to emerge as one that is going wrong. For, in retrospect, comradely attempts to allow space for intellectual growth can appear as no different to lax supervision. How do supervisors learn to manage what might be described as these 'mundane', daily problems of PGR research?

Implications for supervision

- Supervision can represent an exciting and innovative element in an academic portfolio, encompassing a range of tasks that require developmental depth as well as coverage. This makes the educational process a risky one at many levels and puts pressures on the supervisory relationship that can result, on occasions, in a loss of trust on either side. Repairing relationships is not easy, requiring deft interpersonal skills and extensive experience on the part of supervisors in particular.
- Central to supervision and the PhD are relationships with specific areas of knowledge construction or disciplinary fields, whose discourses hold strong implications for what constitutes an acceptable supervisory style. Researcher-teachers should acknowledge the socialization element in supervision in reproducing research communities, whether or not doctoral students intend to become academics. Mature supervision requires recognition of when one is unthinkingly reproducing old, unhelpful, practices and which old practices remain essential to PhD success in your discipline.
- Within the systems, frameworks and codes of practice drawn up in recent years, it is easy to lose sight of postgraduate research education as being about intellectual development and growth. Asking where learning takes place in the PhD means positioning research education as a form of intellectual development and raises questions as to the nature of teaching in a supervisory relationship. Many in universities are uncomfortable with being perceived as teachers, defining themselves primarily as researchers or scholars in relation to their area of study. This does not mean that there is not great pride in standards of teaching; rather that expertise offered to students is seen as arising out of research identities and mastery of subject area.

- An educational approach requires recognition of the complexity of the teaching role – as tutor, guide, mentor, instructor – not least because people (both supervisors and students) do not grow and learn at the same pace or, indeed, uniformly steadily. The needs and skills of both sides will be various and change over the time of a PhD. The transformational elements in doctoral education may not happen to order: imagination and breakthroughs in understanding have their place alongside mundane slog in enabling progress in research projects. Fitting an educational model of teaching into current frameworks and pressure for timely completion is, in some senses, about enabling the messy, creative parts of student development – hence, it is about managing risk and risk-taking.
- By placing risk at the centre of the enterprise, instead of conceptualizing it as an occasional by-product of theses that go wrong, it becomes less fearful and, instead, can be seen an opportunity for creative innovation and as a variety of problems that require solutions. Research students may or may not go through personal and academic-related crises about career ambitions, over their projects, over the purposes of study. But they are unlikely to avoid intellectual crises at all, with a smooth progression from start to finish. What kind of supervisor individuals make depends on their clarity about their own personal strengths and weaknesses under pressure, the disciplinary influences shaping their style and a sense of how to approach crises.
- Are intellectual crises treated as the end-of-the-road, as a failing on the part of the student or the supervisor, or as problems that might be solved? How supervisors and students feel about managing doctoral crises, whether interpersonal or academic, will influence outcomes. Risk is about change: academic crises precipitate innovation, personal development and progression, which do not always come about through careful, safe application to study alone. Dealing with change and crisis is hard and can be experienced as destabilizing: it is how crises are managed that matters, not their avoidance.

The PhD is a tough degree: complicated and demanding; and, indeed, would anyone expect a higher award to be easy? The PhD remains, fundamentally, a research degree, although changes in the last two decades have added to its possible forms (such as doctoral programmes and workplace-based doctorates). Whatever its origins, it is now, *within* academe, about developing knowledge in a specific subject area and its methods and methodology of research. A critical commentary, part of the originality asked of from a successful PhD, sits alongside theorizing the nature and form of knowledge in that subject group and the contribution of the thesis to that group's knowledge-base. It is a risky enterprise for both students and supervisors, for no one can guarantee a successful outcome no matter how good the student or supervisor's prior record. It is an examination, so should be bounded by transparent rules and acceptable to current experts in a subject area – yet the PhD is meant to provide a contribution to knowledge, so should simultaneously live at the riskier edges of its discipline.

Supervising Social and Academic Practices in a Political Context

2

Chapter Outline

A variety of scenarios are presented in this chapter to illustrate the, so far, abstract discussions of contradictory tensions, organizational pressures and competing authority structures impacting on supervision. Some common academic challenges are discussed concerning expectations, tacit knowledge in PhD examination, paradigm clashes, supporting the development of thesis writing, finishing drafts, and becoming socialized into academe via disciplinary-specific practices.

Insider assumptions within universities about the purposes of the PhD have had to accommodate external pressures, for the PhD is no longer only about what people from within universities think. We have seen in Chapter 1 that the quality and success of the postgraduate research students' (PGR) experience has become a matter of concern to governments and funding bodies in particular. The needs of employers in the 'knowledge economy' and the imperative to account for public funds are but two of the powerful drivers that have opened up university practices in doctoral education to examination in the 1980s and 1990s.

Taylor and Beasley (2005) describe how the PhD's fortunes rose with governments' quests for economic growth and defence developments from the

1960s onward (p. 9); but, from the 1990s onwards, suffered from dependence on government funding in an era of cutbacks and accountability for public spending (pp. 9–16). Annan (1999) viewed the extraordinary and rapid changes to which universities in the UK have been subject from the well-established angle of Oxford and Cambridge, yet even from this supposedly solid perspective, he commented that at the end of the Thatcher years 'the dons no longer inhabited a stable and autonomous world. They had to bend to the political winds' (p. 298).

These wider changes are reflected in pressures on universities since the 1980s arising from governments' requirements for more accountability in exchange for public funds. The national Quality Assurance Agency's (QAA) code of practice (www.qaa.ac.uk/academicinfrastructure/codeOfPractice/) and public league tables of success (www.hefce.ac.uk) are now a part of the scenery for both supervisors and students. National university league tables based on a range of activities produce varied results according to whose criteria predominate. The post-Research Assessment Exercise (RAE) metrics for evaluating institutional research success (now called REF, 'Research Excellence Framework'), too, include a university's record in relation to PhD supervision.

The QAA's national code of practice for higher education includes a section on postgraduate research which is generally reflected in formalized quality processes at institutional level. However, while supervisors are accustomed to local teaching quality assurance and enhancement processes at undergraduate and Master's levels, supervisory teaching primarily arises out of research identities in ways that makes its links to local frameworks unclear and irksome to some (although by no means all). The international nature of research communities does not protect from the need to conform to local teaching practices and codes arising from external or stakeholder pressure. Harley *et al.* (2004) argue that increased fragmentation of roles due to a privileging of academic research activity is linked to increased managerialism:

> . . . the measurement of research productivity in terms of performance indicators linked to funding has given the employing organization much more interest in and control over academic work than has hitherto been the case, at all levels of the academic hierarchy. (p. 336)

As a visiting trainer of supervisors I have observed the expression of supervisors' rage at what they perceive to be their local administrators' instigation of rules about supervision.

Tensions arise within academic departments and institutions as research supervision comes further under the management of what can appear as locally initiated systems and which, to some, miss key elements in doctoral education. Most notably, pressure for timely completion has become the key element in which internal and external pressures combine and influence individual supervisors. So, for example, Whitelock *et al.* (2008) have argued that education for creativity (arising from collaborative interaction, especially between student and supervisors) is overlooked in recent research and supervisor training agendas, even though creativity and originality remain central goals in doctoral education. They argue that, rather than focusing only on technical and craft skills, novice researchers require supervisors with time and expertise to build up the trust necessary for 'collaborative creativity'. Supervisory meetings, then, can reflect a myriad of expectations and pressures drawn from both inside and outside universities, and result in different levels of interpersonal, institutional and inter-agency tension impacting on them.

Trying to make sense of these (sometimes competing) expectations, unravelling the layers, is an essential part of my work in trying to support research students. Since the 1980s I have worked with students facing some level of challenge with their studies – my work includes teaching courses, workshops and individual tutorials for research students as well as undergraduates and taught postgraduates, plus I have been running courses for supervisors since 2000. It is never easy to discern from the outside exactly what the nature of a supervisory or research problem is or what the best approaches to it should be. A crisis or problem, in this context, is taken as being some combination of intellectual, cognitive and affective dilemmas that are halting progress and that need to be solved in order to proceed.

In broad terms, students learn (or do not learn) to negotiate social and academic practices within a supervisory framework that requires a level of trust and understanding, yet within an institutional context where the balance of power and control is not always easily understood. Some 'factional' scenarios follow, describing themes that problems commonly group around. As with all my examples, students and staff are not recognizable because these scenarios represent a combination of research and situations I meet regularly rather than specific, historical events. They illustrate issues surrounding: (1) expectations; (2) tacit knowledge and negotiating the PhD as an examination; (3) paradigm clashes and interdisciplinarity; (4) supporting writing in academe; (5) working with academic dispositions; (6) finishing draft theses; and (7) becoming an academic.

A crisis of expectations?

A student has come to see me because he is dissatisfied with his supervisor and is not sure where to go for help in getting his supervisor to become better at the role. He is not happy with the outcome of supervisory meetings and, additionally, feels that his supervisor does not allow him sufficient time. I ask what he would like the meetings to achieve and in what ways they currently fail to do what he wants.

He is, first, offended by his supervisor's lack of social skills: he does not expect friendship, but had expected some level of interest in him as a human being. He has begun to feel that his supervisor neither knows nor cares how he is getting on. Meetings happen only when the student insists; he has no sense that he is entitled to a regular slot in his supervisors' timetable. The student has had a successful career in public sector management roles at home (he is an international student) and is at a loss with a supervisor who has difficulty making eye contact (there are, of course, great cultural variations about the appropriateness of eye contact). Most infuriatingly, his supervisor can never make a decision: whenever asked by the student 'should I do X or Y?', his supervisor says 'what do you think?' 'Why would I ask him, if I knew?' is the student's exasperated response.

There are clearly competing views about the roles of students and supervisors in this relationship. I have met the supervisor, and wonder how much their exchanges are both driving each other into becoming cartoons of themselves: the student becoming increasingly pushy and extrovert, and the supervisor increasingly withdrawn and introverted. I am aware that:

- Students who travel half way round the world to study are often highly committed to what they believe the educational experience will bring them.
- People who pay large amounts of money do not like to be made to feel that they are a nuisance.
- Conceptualizing 'failing' as an option is especially painful for people who have disrupted their families and their careers in order to be students.

But I am also aware:

- That some supervisors feel immensely uncomfortable when faced with apparently dependent behaviour – which represents 'non-academic' behaviour (echoing Bendix's description of 'other').
- 'Reflective questioning' is sometimes considered to be a tool for encouraging independence in student thinking.

- A student who presents as unhappy and frustrated can appear to be demanding at a personal level, which is not necessarily the supervisor's area of expertise (where they may feel confident in solving research problems).

There is a breakdown of belief and understanding between these two (see Chapter 1 for Hockey's notion of losing trust), and numerous tacit expectations on both sides about appropriate behaviour. While, at one level, intellectual capacity is deemed to be inherent (or not) in students, nonetheless socially acquired behaviours and dispositions are the signals by which ability is recognized, and these are usually shaped by notions of what an academic is (whether or not the student intends to become a professional intellectual). Frustration has grown between these two, with misunderstanding on both sides. It is not clear yet where the research topic sits in this confusion or the extent to which progress in the research itself is seriously impeded by the state of the student-supervisor relationship.

Tacit knowledge: negotiating the PhD as an examination

On the train, travelling home from examining a thesis, I wonder if there could be a way in which vivas or internal review panels could be a pain-free experience. The viva is a major event, the culmination of at least three years' work (often more), probably about 70,000 words and much sacrifice. A lot rides on it, yet no one can guarantee the outcome. It is a testing exam. It need not be long, but the questions asked are likely to be probing and difficult. A wise student does some preparation. The viva requires the art of coping with criticism constructively, seeing the logic in how it arises, discussing it coherently and – where necessary – arguing and defending one's ground. So rather than getting heated when challenged, a cool head and reflective thought under pressure are useful attributes.

Strong nerves are also useful: for waiting beforehand, but also – towards the end of the viva – when asked to wait outside the exam room for the examiners' decision. While the student is waiting, the examiners may well be taking time to put a clear list of changes together so that there is absolute clarity about the outcome. Among those waiting will be at least one supervisor. It is hard as a supervisor (especially as a new supervisor) not to feel under examination along with the candidate. A natural sense of responsibility for such a big part of a student's life, coupled with lack of control over the outcome is an uncomfortable mix. Further, although able to guide students in various directions, one cannot write the thesis or make substantive breakthroughs in understanding on their behalf – just illuminate the path in front of them. It is highly likely that a tired student (desperate to get the PhD out of their life) will be asked to do more work.

It matters, then, what state of mind both supervisors and students are in when approaching vivas, and a dollop of discomfort seems to be an inevitable ingredient. Students who approach vivas and review panels as a process of negotiation are in a strong position. They are more likely to encompass the viva as another step further along the path: often receiving the promise of a doctorate if they make specific changes (where, before, no promise of a doctorate existed). Students who approach vivas in a state of desperation, believing it to be the end-point of the journey, are in a vulnerable place if changes are required. Trust, not just between supervisors and students, but between them and the system itself, is at a premium.

Examining has the potential to encompass those moments that are sometimes tainted by baser human emotions and relationships. Pearce (2005) has provided fictional case studies summarizing problems that occur sufficiently regularly to be recognizable: the nit-picking examiner, the jealous colleague attacking the supervisor via the student, and 'foul play' in which the external feels set up by the situation (pp.2–7, 2005). Tinkler and Jackson (2004) suggest that candidates' accounts of examiners' agendas may be shaped by not knowing the examiners' intentions behind questions and by candidates' own emotions attached to the viva. Nonetheless, their data from candidates reinforce 'accounts from academics which suggest that some examiners are motivated by non-academic agendas' (p. 39). Supervisors are engaged in a range of power relations: within their international research reference group, as well as locally within their employing department. Where they stand in these groups may well shape the ways in which they feel able to influence the success or otherwise of their students. As Morley *et al.* have argued, the viva itself is 'a major relay of power' with gatekeeping as well as educational functions (p. 271). The elements that they describe as the micropolitics of the viva can equally well be argued to be present in the lead-up to final assessment, reflected in departmental review panels and local upgrade procedures. While these are usually seen as effective ways of ensuring good supervision they can also reflect what Morley *et al.* describe:

> . . . viva stories that permeate academe give accounts of students being negatively affected by power struggles between the supervisor and the external examiner,

or of theses which some might consider quality products being failed as a result of a clash of values. Feminist scholarship, for example, can be ridiculed by unsympathetic examiners; interdisciplinary work can be inappropriately examined; and international students treated as second-class citizens. (p. 271)

Resilience and capacity to defend one's thesis are tested in a viva, hence part of the achievement lies in managing the challenges inherent in such an exercise. Systems, too, have changed, to include non-examining colleagues to chair the meeting, to allow for the possibility of tape-recording vivas and for the presence of supervisors. All are means of introducing a public eye into what used to be a relatively private matter in the UK – thereby curbing the excesses of the occasional odd examiner.

Like Delamont *et al.* and Morley *et al.*, Sinclair (1997) draws on Bourdieu's notions of 'habitus' and 'dispositions' to develop a framework for analysing 'making doctors'. Sinclair's view of 'dispositions' in the professional education of doctors is a useful basis from which to conceptualize 'academic dispositions' as family resemblances in behaviour and attributes required in academe (to avoid becoming Bendix's 'other') regardless of students' career intentions. Sinclair writes:

> The habitus is the collectively created sum of infinitely variable (though organized) mental and physical manifestations of dispositions, as embodied in individual people. So, while the constituent dispositions of a group of people may be the same, the way in which each individual practises them is different, depending on each individual's own experience and 'style'. (p. 20)

And, one might add, according to specific context: so resilience and capacity to defend one's thesis may be expressed slightly differently in different disciplines or subject groups, perhaps with greater or lesser degrees of robustness or aggression.

Paradigm clashes and academic positioning

The power games that surround academic hierarchies can be difficult to negotiate, and the academic enterprise includes jostling for place in a subject area or discipline. Establishing one's own position within an academic debate can mean taking issue with prior knowledge and conceptualization – and others will hit back. The academic dispositions required include intellectual clarity and, sometimes, courage to mark out one's ground and defend it. A part of expressing intellectual clarity is achieved by careful argumentation and persuasive evidencing of one's thesis.

I am sitting in a tutorial with a PhD student who is looking for help because she has not produced any written work of value for six months. Apart from a number of small papers and an amount of data analysis, she appears not to be making the progress she and her supervisor are hoping for at this stage. The student is pale, voice monotonous and she describes herself as both lazy and disorganized.

I offer the traditional invitation: tell me about your PhD. This opens a range of possibilities: a description of the experience so far, the title, the explanation that 'you won't understand'. In this case it produced a question, 'what is there to know?' Interesting that, not 'what would you like to know?' but something more damning. 'What would you like to tell me?' felt too aggressive a response in the circumstances, so I suggested she tell me the story of how she got into it, how she chose her topic and how it has been so far. Her face lightened as she explained how she came to choose her topic – it had clearly enthused her at one point.

A social science student, there was the common tale of muddle as she had changed supervisors. The supervisor she had intended to study with had been 'poached' by another university for the RAE, and she was now with the 'second' supervisor plus another new lecturer (early in his career, supportive and kind but no match for the sharp-shooting number one supervisor). There had been struggles around agreeing data collection and she had compromised, agreeing to include a questionnaire as well as carrying out interviews. With an amount of rewriting, the last review panel had agreed that she should proceed into her third year on condition she produced a chapter-by-chapter outline of her thesis. Once this had been done, she had not written a word of the thesis itself.

Now the scene is set, I ask her to tell me what she wants to say in her thesis, to tell me what the main messages are. Her answer is to tell me what data she has collected. How does it fit into the existing literature in the field? Bit by bit it becomes evident that qualitative data is allowing her to map out arguments that seem to be relatively new in the field – or at least to take issue with some key concepts. She is less interested in the questionnaire data, although this does reinforce her arguments. Her current first supervisor is only interested in the questionnaire data, and wants the interview material to be used as illustrative of the questionnaire findings.

From where I am sitting I do not know if:

- Arguing with her supervisor (and hence taking issue with major figures in the field) is in some way inhibiting her writing.
- If the supervisor is leading her in a direction that will ensure success in the PhD, rather than allowing a riskier direction in which success may be in doubt.
- If her supervisor just does not recognize the research paradigm within which the student is making sense of her work.

Experience tells me that it could be any of these individually, or a mixture of all three. It is clear that the chapter outline is acting as a straightjacket for the student, while acting as an essential ingredient for the review panel to recognize the PhD potential of her work.

The HEFCE report on student completion echoes Delamont *et al* (see Chapter 1) in its comments on methodological wrangling, noting that some social science and humanities subjects (with lower completion rates than natural science subjects) 'are not always so well established as in the natural sciences and methodologies may still be disputed' (2005, p. 34, para. 118). Theorizing is a central part of a successful PhD in a number of ways: one (in many, but not all, subjects) is in methodology – the philosophy or rationale underpinning the *choice* of methods used. The second area is in the overall theorizing of one's data or argument and how this relates to existing major debates in the most relevant areas, as well as to one's research questions. These two are interlinked, signalling what is accepted as knowledge and evidence in an area of study – hence methods that are contentious in some disciplines can be subject to feuds. What are laid out as apparently rational and logical choices about data collection and analysis often represent passionately held beliefs and act, indirectly, as signs of group membership or attempts to enlist with particular groups. Whether or not the student intends to become a professional academic as a career choice, this process of 'becoming' a group member shapes the PhD experience. So, for example, in social science subjects the choices between using statistics or qualitative methods can signal positioning in relation to a major schism.

Students, however, often occupy 'cross-disciplinary' and 'interdisciplinary' spaces between and across groups. Within broad subject groupings, not all academics are clearly in one camp or another, but positioned on a continuum that represents the dominant feud. Hence, for students, how to position oneself as a novice researcher in relation to an obvious (international) academic reference group is not always clear. Fortunately, though, some students manage this process with relative ease. Learning to manage supervisors and internal review panels helps students to rehearse the skills needed for vivas – including how to choose and defend their positioning. However, from time to time supervisors and reviewers will not consider positioning that falls outside their own stance, and understand this not as a paradigm clash but as a failing on the part of students.

Supporting academic writing

My social science student, struggling with academic positioning, had discussed with her supervisor the potential usefulness of visiting me, and they had agreed between them that I would be asked to give her advice on time-management and act as 'overseer' to ensure she did certain amounts of writing every week. However, what Morley *et al.* call a 'technicist' approach (see Introduction) is not necessarily sufficient to achieve a successful PhD, in which entry to networks is via powerful gatekeepers and which needs to be negotiated intellectually during the process of writing. These problems may materialize through writing, in which case splitting two such tasks between two sets of support is highly likely to prove unproductive. A 'techniques' approach to writing can sometimes help progress and sometimes it can be a hindrance, and it takes trial and error to decide what is an appropriate approach at a given moment in time.

Developing trust in one's own writing patterns as a student is not easy when under pressure to produce a completed PhD, and it is hard for supervisors to stand by and watch when time is of the essence. The pressure to complete the thesis looms so large that it can, on occasions, get in the way of completion, and students find themselves on the receiving end of a variety of advice and demands. So, for example, like this student, people may be required to write chapter outlines before they have solved the intellectual problems from which such an index would arise; the writing and wording of research questions must be set before data is collected, and this becomes a matter of dogma, even if the agreed methods require an iterative approach; and the writing of each chapter is demanded in order, especially producing a polished first chapter before moving onto the rest.

Occasionally, a supervisor will insist that a student approach writing in a particular way or a particular order because they believe it is the right way to do things, or because it has worked for them: 'This is how I work, this is how my colleagues work, so this is the way you must work.' It can be a relief for some students to be given clear instructions in a complicated process, but relief may be limited if such directions are experienced as deskilling, with the complexity of writing remaining a mystery over which others seem to have control. Not surprisingly, supervisors with clear rules in their heads about how to write are unlikely, when their competence is judged by their students' timely completions, to find the patience to wait while students develop individual solutions to their writing problems.

One science PhD student was well advanced in data collection, analysis and presentation of papers at conferences and seminars, but found that the PhD itself was not forthcoming. Their supervisor insisted that the first chapter should be written before writing any other chapters, after producing a full outline for the contents page; and, like many scientists, believed that writing-up was something that needed to be considered only at the end of the whole PhD process. The student could not produce Chapter 1 because the rest of the thesis was not yet clear to them, and indeed had become thoroughly blocked.

The student easily gave me: an overview of what their research was about; the research questions being addressed and why; what data had been collected; how and why it had been analysed the way it had; what the main findings and key messages were; and how all of this fitted into the literature. All the ingredients were, then, ready and waiting to be combined into a thesis. I reverted to an old approach: ask the student to present a rough idea of how many chapters they think they will write, given what is usual in their discipline. I draw a picture of the pretend thesis and sketch in what, roughly, each chapter might be doing, for example:

Intro – literature	literature	Methods & methodology	Data/analysis
Data/analysis	Data/analysis	Data/analysis	Discussion & conclusions

In this case, the logical order of the data chapters was clear because of the kinds of experimental work carried out; plus, conference and seminar papers, and recent analysis provided material for chapters. We agreed then, that copies of relevant material would be cut and pasted into 'pretend' chapters, to be later shaped into real chapters, with the overall thesis linking them together to make a draft. That way, it was possible to produce Chapter 1, but only once the 'pretend PhD' had led to a full draft.

Sadly, the student felt a need to do this secretly and was anxious that the supervisor did not know that a different approach to writing had been taken, hence confirming the supervisor's belief that their approach to teaching writing is one that works well in all circumstances.

Finishing drafts

I am sitting with an arts student who has attended many of my courses during the time of his PhD. He is struggling to understand why it is that he cannot write, given that he just has to finish the last chapter to have a whole draft of a PhD. I know that he works hard and is committed to finishing: he is focused, organized and very, very bright. Yet he is shocked by the painful force with which this 'writing block' has kicked in.

To bystanders, it seems to be a matter of commonsense that all the rewards of completing a PhD are close to hand if he would only let completion happen. The compelling nature of this viewpoint can make it hard for non-completers to hear the contents of their own heads. As chance would have it, I was being treated for back problems when I was trying to finish my thesis: I was seeing a sports' specialist, whose matter-of-fact conversations as she worked reflected a sports' specialist's awareness of the phenomenon of talented, hard-working athletes who could never quite win the big events. This helped normalize my feelings which, like many others, I had assumed to be a set of destructive emotions peculiar to myself. Of course, there can be as many reasons for writing blocks as there are people, and awareness does not always equal finding a way through these blockages. However, having some sense of why this (almost physical) barrier to progress has erupted into life can at least return a sense of order and reason to life, where students have previously begun to doubt their own sanity.

Finishing a draft opens up, for students, the unnerving possibility of a viva. Plus, supervisors often return drafts with large quantities of criticism, in order to show how to take the draft forward to become a PhD. A tired student can lose faith at this point, and can hear the supervisors' comments as meaning 'this is hopeless'. How criticism resonates can depend on the student's emotional state concerning finishing, and the transitions that inevitably surround giving up being a graduate student. The act of stating one's argument and positioning it in relation to existing academic debates can be alarming. For me, the prospect of being awarded a PhD included giving up the identity of someone who was not successful academically. While a negative identity could be seen as little enough to lose, nonetheless all changes of identity include painful risks, and there is comfort in staying with what is known.

While I give people plenty of time to talk aloud about their feelings, to put some order into what feels like chaos, I do not analyse these emotions. Rather, my role is to work 'alongside' as people face up to writing again, and the bad news is that it is about learning how to work gently through the discomfort that accompanies writing blocks, little by little. It requires human support and understanding, not judgement.

Becoming an academic: ownership of knowledge within a hierarchy

A social science student, whose research is mainly carried out in their own workplace, describes the difficulties of building up trust within the hierarchical, competitive environment of universities. He is explaining in tones of frustration how hopeless his supervisory team is as a team. The main supervisor is an academic of international renown, who made it plain from the outset that 'joint' supervision required by the institution was of no interest to her and that meetings of all three together would be a waste of time. The academic dispositions associated with success in the field meant that the main supervisor was excellent at providing information about and entrée to networks, conferences and knowledge of recent publications. The student also had the impression that she had examined PhDs in the area recently. She barely tolerated the junior co-supervisor, dismissing his suggestions for research design and suggesting the student consult with the co-supervisor if he was 'upset' or needed his 'hand holding'.

As a successful and high-flying manager himself, the student had read the signs to mean that when the second supervisor did not fight back then he was a junior, less able supervisor. So, early on, he took the hint and only consulted the main supervisor. But now he had to present his work to a departmental panel for review, his main supervisor was abroad (travelling on sabbatical) and his second supervisor said he had not been consulted sufficiently to feel able to read the student's papers at short notice. He was at a loss as to how to manage the review panel in the absence of supervisory advice.

What is not always obvious to graduate students is how hierarchical universities are and so they only rarely understand easily their supervisors' working environments and its pressures. It is no longer quite as stultifying as the days when staff were divided into college dons or college servants: universities are numerous and varied in style, size and history, and this is reflected in their structures. At heart, however, life is still split into academic, administrative and support staff, the latter two categories covering a range of hierarchies of their own. Universities are highly competitive environments, and while not uniformed as in an army, nonetheless jobs are ranked. Full-time, non-temporary lecturers may expect to progress through lectureship grades to senior lectureships and eventually to professorial level. Research, publications and teaching are key ingredients in the competition for promotion (although the balance of these varies from university to university); and these activities are coupled with administrative responsibility. While the balance between teaching and research varies according to institution, historically the construction of knowledge has not always been central to progression: Annan assumed 'dons' to be defined by their teaching activities in Oxford or Cambridge colleges and a few elite institutions (in London, LSE, Imperial, University College, plus leading civic universities) and to be without commitment to ideas or intellectualism (p. 5).

Currently, however, what Harley *et al.* have called 'privileging of academic research' means that research has become key to certain kinds of professional success, as the medium for jostling for position in national and international disciplinary research groups within which one displays ownership of ideas and knowledge in a specific, focused area of study. This autonomous academic identity requires confidence in intellectual ownership and decision-making, which is not necessarily the same as being an extrovert performer and teacher. Becoming known for specialist scholarship and research and building a reputation within at least one cross-institutional community comes via attendance at conferences, presenting papers and publishing regularly within that sphere. In addition, researchers need to become involved in successful bidding for research funds or joining, and establishing or taking forward a research network.

Key relationships in research, then, lie outside the home institution. The carbon footprints of successful academics reflect high levels of travel, to conferences and to teach, to visit and to give papers. While being the individual expert within an institution, they link to relevant outside networks without through travel, through publications, through meetings and through the internet. They are, then, both the owner of an area of knowledge within their institution and a group member outside of this. The dispositions required to become a central member of international research communities include confidence, clarity, the capacity to argue one's corner convincingly and an adversarial energy that takes issue with other scholars.

My student's supervisory relationships may have been easier to manage in a science team, where the roles of main supervisor and post-doc supervisors are better established. But in the arts and social sciences, it is possible for supervisor to see joint teams as an infringement of their 'master' status and ownership of that piece of the research field. The student fears that by throwing in his lot with one supervisor, the second supervisor has developed a sense of grievance which is leaving the student unsupported and unadvised during the review process.

Implications for supervision

- Learning trust and understanding for both students and supervisors sits at a point where interpersonal expectations meet an educational arena shaped by a range of social and academic pressures. The PhD encompasses complexities in academic life: the elements in the mix include risk, power, competition, epistemology and ownership of knowledge. Recent changes have led to systemic attempts to manage the PhD's inherent riskiness and these can run the danger of limiting opportunities for idiosyncratic, creative developments over time. Yet not attempting to manage risk within quality frameworks can leave the supervisor and the student feeling exposed and vulnerable. Both students and supervisors need to get to know their local rules and regulations, systems and processes for managing progression and learn how to make them work as supports rather than seeing them as barriers.
- Developing trust between students and supervisors and the system they are all working in takes time and effort. For supervisors, recognizing the pathway that underpins progression in their discipline provides a route map that removes much mystery – for example, end-of-first term review, confirmation of PhD status (and what is required for this), planning an achievable project in the time available, gaining access to data, experiments, ethical approval, and end-of-year reviews are standard stages in doctoral education.
- Recognition that individuals vary hugely in how they learn, develop and adjust to challenge requires supervisors to be flexible in how they approach supervisory tasks. However, this is a delicate balancing act that has to be set against supervisors' personal understanding, time constraints and demands of the research process. Given that the PhD is an educational process, support for students in accessing their personal resilience and strength to meet disciplinary based challenges is to be preferred over the unthinking repetition of old or brutalizing practices.
- It is easy to forget as a supervisor how students experience power relations in university systems. While systemically, attempts are made to recalibrate power imbalances (such as arrangements made for vivas – independent chairs and recordings), nonetheless students are entering their supervisors' territories (who act as gatekeepers to wider research communities) and are subject to their judgements and those of examiners. It is for supervisors to be aware of the social practices and expressions of academic dispositions operating in their field, and their interplay with developing academic practices. This may range from needing to unpick tacit knowledge about what is expected at any given moment to supporting students as they learn to manage paradigm clashes evident in departmental review panels.

The pedagogical problem, set within this framework of cross-cutting pressures, is to find ways of supporting individual students' development in the time available; to work in ways that help students face up to challenges and academic crises within the chosen disciplinary discourse. This is, of course, a joint endeavour between students and supervisors: but it is an intellectually complex experience and one that, on the road to successful completion, provides both supervisors and students with plenty of opportunities for miscommunication and misunderstanding.

Part 2
Key Perspectives

Part 2 considers supervision and the experience of the PhD from a range of key perspectives: successful PhD completers; current PhD students; and university professionals and academic managers who work with PGR students and supervisors in administrative, managerial and support roles.

In Chapter 3, we see that successful PhD completers emphasized the personal nature of their success. They valued good supervision, but their accounts stressed the importance of personal qualities in overcoming the difficulties of the PhD. Change was an important theme in describing their experiences: change in themselves and in supervision.

The individualized and experiential nature of the PhD is most clearly illustrated by the responses and accounts of current students, which are explored in Chapter 4. Their uncertainty about final outcomes and management of research challenges illustrate how the PhD remains both a major achievement and a tough exercise.

Chapter 5 examines the views of a variety of university staff in administrative, support and managerial roles. Their tasks, for example, of mediation and of monitoring institutional completion rates, are reflected in a belief in the need for systemic solutions and an awareness of how external drivers could change the nature of supervision.

Completing: Slaying the Dragon

3

Chapter Outline

'Completion' is explored in this chapter in its wider sense as a vantage point for understanding students' educational experience and as the change of mindset this can represent. The question asked is: what do the PhD and supervision look like to those who have succeeded? Data from 19 graduates provided a sense of the experience of supervision from the perspective of students who had achieved successful outcomes. Accounts used in this chapter include both good and bad experiences in which the good never outweighs bad (even in the light of success). Participants in the study emphasized the importance of their personal qualities and characteristics in achieving successful completion.

So far, supervision and the PhD have been presented as positioned within a context of multiple pressures: national (e.g. funding bodies, QAA precepts), international (disciplinary research discourses and communities) and institutional (departmental, faculty, school, unit or whole-university regulations and practices). Within this macro framework, completion of a successful PhD has dominated recent discussions and across any one institution, completion arises from a jigsaw of interlocking pieces:

- Administration and regulations – for example, being able to track students accurately during their time of registration and having regulations that back up a three-four year finishing goal for full-time students.

- Project planning and progression management – if the work is not planned as a three year project and problems are not addressed along the way, then a full-time degree is unlikely to finish within the timeframe.
- Quality of supervision – including relevant and appropriate workload allocation models, joint or supervisory teams and training to develop supervisors' skills and insight into the PhD process.
- Student motivation – keeping interest and morale over a long period of time is challenging whether full time, part time or on doctoral programmes, whether international students or UK and in full-time work.
- Training and development opportunities for students in specific research and transferable skills, plus attendance at conferences and events.
- Student experience – it is not possible to make such a challenging degree free from problems, however a sense of welcome into an academic community via contact (if a distance student) and events, or, for example, via PGR spaces in university buildings for full-time and visiting students can contribute to a positive experience.

But, while this detailed jigsaw provides the essential backdrop to doctoral education, it does not tell us about the *nature* of completion as an educational stage that students and supervisors have to negotiate and experience. For some years I have been running groups and workshops for 'finishing' students. A common question is: why not just put on a website what it is students need to know and let them get on with it? The key assumption in this question is that students are not finishing because they lack awareness of what the final stages look like. While there are 'tick box' elements to finishing, knowing the steps does not provide the 'transformational' elements of courage, confidence, energy and capacity to manage projects and supervisors that the experience of completing a thesis can demand. Elsewhere (Peelo 1994, 2002), I have argued that learning development needs to pay attention to the cognitive, social and affective aspects of learning, and PhD education is no different in these respects. Ahern and Manathunga (2004) likewise describe the importance of the social, affective and cognitive aspects of 'clutch-starting stalled research students', and summarize how blockages can relate to: avoidance, anxiety, self-sabotage, fear of failure, motivation, low self-esteem, differences with supervisors and framing of the PhD task.

Feelings around completion, in my experience, arise from a wide range of possible relationships with, for example, oneself (e.g. as an achiever), with academe, with futures and transitions, and with discomfort at moving into a stage in which one is examined in a relatively public arena. In contrast, completion is sometimes framed as the smooth and inevitable outcome of a properly managed process. There is some truth in the notion that a badly planned project cannot be completed in the time available and Trafford and Leshem (2008) have argued that by understanding the viva (i.e. the logical endpoint) from the start makes the PhD more attainable. While accepting this notion up to a point, I have increasingly begun to frame completion as a change of mindset that requires students to throw themselves into the final stages (however frightened, unconfident or ambivalent they feel). Once everything else is in place (e.g. project design, management, equipment and supervision, data collection, understanding and relevant academic development) then two elements are required for successful completion: the desire to get the PhD out of one's life once and for all; and the belief that successful completion is possible.

The nineteen completers who contributed to this project studied within the same time-span as those in the HEFCE (2005) study of a cohort of students starting PhDs at a UK Higher Education Institute in the academic year 1996–97. What is important about the HEFCE study is that it moves beyond the careers of the full-time, funded research council students alone (who have been central to national debates) and attempts, instead, to look at the whole research student population. HEFCE estimated that just over 19,000 students started in 1996–97: some 14,041 full-time students and 5,150 part-time (p. 8). 369 full-timers did not go beyond Year 1, and 299 part-timers likewise (p. 8). They estimated completion rates for the cohort to be: 71 per cent of full-time students had finished after seven years (57 per cent after five years) and 37 per cent of part-time students had completed after seven years (19 per cent after five years) (see p. 3).

Part-time completers, then, represent a relatively small group; yet even among full-time students, nearly 30 per cent have not completed within seven years. While full time and part time is never easy to chart accurately (people start as full time and move to part time, and vice versa over the course of their degrees), over 60 per cent of part-timers have still to complete at seven years. Time taken to complete, of itself, need not always be problematic intellectually or educationally and some part-time students may wish their PhDs to be long-term (sometimes, unfairly, described as 'hobby' PhDs). However, given the speed with which knowledge advances, some PhDs will become impossible to complete with the passing of time, due to changes in disciplinary discourses and understanding of the topic.

I chose as my starting point for exploring student perspectives to look at those who had, ultimately, succeeded in their goal of gaining a PhD. Perhaps I was still at the stage of naively hoping that successful PhDs equal successful supervision. This was mistaken, of course, because the graduates portrayed in this chapter had experienced what they saw as both good and bad supervision, and the bad had not stopped them succeeding even when they felt it had slowed them down or reduced confidence. In terms of the PhD as a good experience, this group valued learning new skills, making new contacts, being at the 'cutting edge', acquiring knowledge, developing greater self-knowledge and meeting mental and physical challenges. The negatives included: toil, slog, isolation, fear, a sense of overwhelming pressure, neglectful supervision and frustration.

As a provider of supervision courses, I have become increasingly alert to the dangers inherent in constructing 'interesting' case studies that represent situations which have gone dramatically wrong, as my recognition has grown that completion is often about a change of student mindset whatever has gone before (good or bad). Logically, of course, it makes sense that such a change of mindset will become more attainable in supportive contexts. But by definition, successful completers have negotiated the academic problems and crises of the PhD: what then, does the PhD and supervision mean from the perspective of success?

Overview of responses

I sent out a highly speculative questionnaire to colleagues around the country, who passed it on to ex-students. What follows is not, in any way, presented as representative of anyone other than the 19 people who chose to respond. Nor were this group of completers prompted with questionnaire items, and no theories drawn from prior research or the literature were tested out; rather, completers were asked simple questions to group their thoughts around, to see what issues would emerge. The completers recounted histories of good supervisors and bad supervisors, family problems and emotional blocks to progress, supervisors moved, life happened – not all vivas were good, and many faced amendments on some scale or another. Yet they all completed.

While PhD students, they had worked in demanding careers, sometimes changing jobs and accommodation. Life was busy: some were becoming parents for the first time, while others had elderly or sick relatives within their families. There were full-time students with research council awards who had been resident at a university with few other distractions, but others did their PhDs as part of a doctoral programme or lived at a distance from the university at which they were registered and studied part time. Nearly all had found something in the PhD experience to be relevant whatever their current employment – even though not all were publishing or continuing to research. Only two saw no relationship at all between their current work and the PhD.

While completion is a category for universities and funding bodies to assess the success of doctoral education, it is rarely a clear-cut moment in time for the student (although graduation obviously is). It is a drawn-out stage of drafting and redrafting a final thesis plus being examined, both of which require a mindset which believes in the possibility of successful completion. Completers in this project talked about progress being made possible by a range of personal characteristics: *'Personal dedication and genuine interest in the research'*; *'Personal drive and ambition'*; *'Sheer bloody-mindedness'*; *'I think also stubbornness and not wanting to fail played a big part.'* This means, of course, taking high levels of responsibility for one's own progress, and this determination to finish was reflected in how some completers had approached the whole of the process, including an element of what might be described as an obsessive and committed approach to research.

When asked about the positives in the experience, they all answered easily – even the angriest. It was clear that when describing the best and worst of experiences, relishing an academic challenge was important to most of these completers. In terms of 'academic dispositions', some characteristics were rehearsed during the PGR experience: a single-minded (almost obsessive) focus on one area of work, determination to continue to the (sometimes bitter) end, an ownership of an area so that one's identity – at least temporarily – becomes entwined with the subject and with finishing the research. What became clear was that this group faced a variety of events and periods in their studies that they experienced as unpleasant. Two, in particular, had unhappy experiences at vivas which led to a prolonged period of rewriting followed by resubmission. These experiences seemed, however, neither to eclipse the good experiences nor to prevent them succeeding. The narratives told were positive, but echoed the ambivalence commented on by Styles and Radloff (2000) in that the emotions recalled were not easy ones, and the struggles recounted still reverberated through their lives. What follows gives a taste of the ways in which these students (1) described their experiences as both good and bad; how they (2) described the experience of being supervised; and (3) the importance of change, both personal and in academic circumstances, as a theme that described students' time as PhD students.

Was it a good or a bad experience?

Overall, this group was highly positive about what they perceived as the good aspects of their PGR experience, and presented positive responses even though it later became clear that they had also undergone episodes they experienced as unpleasant. What was equally clear, however, was that the good never lessened *how* bad it was on occasions, even with the potentially softening effects of hindsight. Neither was everything difficult defined by them as automatically unpleasant. Intellectual challenge was usually seen as positive, whereas bad was construed as any damaging, unpleasant events perceived as unnecessary. Only two completers, one science and one social science, made unqualified positive statements:

> It was a positive experience as I gained many skills and made lots of contacts.
> I had a wonderful experience because I had brilliant supervision and I was studying a subject that I really loved. I had previously spent ten years in the NHS so it was great to do something for me!

Another two teetered on the edge of unqualified positivity, but tempered it with 'never again'. Perhaps they were just more positive versions of what the bulk of respondents said, describing the experience as a two-edged sword; for example, one arts student commented, '*I loved the work; the actual "student" experience was crap.*'

Life shaped the PhD experience. Most found their PhD to be challenging intellectually, but this satisfying challenge fitted into lives already full with paid work, family commitments, plus sometimes working at a distance from their PGR institution. Not surprisingly, these competing commitments influenced their view of the PhD experience, as one social scientist commented:

> Good – the knowledge and skills being acquired made me feel good. The feeling of working at the cutting edge of a subject made me feel good . . . It was long and hard. I was not able to concentrate fully upon up, do it, and get it out of the way. It had to fit in around work demands and family needs.

They were highly aware of the absence of a supportive academic community around them. One part-time science student working away from their institution illustrated the assumptions they made about what was missing:

> It was good, I enjoyed the challenge and the work. Writing was hard for me, but perseverance helps! . . . I was working and researching 200 miles from my university. I had very little interaction with other research students, just my supervisors. This could have been better but wasn't practically possible in my situation.

Devenish *et al.* (2009) have argued that the value of informal, relational work to successful doctoral education is hidden from universities if they define too narrowly the stages to completion. The quality of the experience, the sense of being valued and belonging that comes from peer support, in their experience, contributes to successful PhDs.

Whereas another science student intimated that the drive to complete meant that 'good' and 'bad' experiences were irrelevant categories when it came to part-time completion:

> Because of my particular circumstances, I didn't feel like a PGR student; I was doing a job and fitting in my PhD around it, and to that extent it was very, very tiring and could be quite frustrating at times when I was not able to continue with my doctoral work due to pressure of work. The pressure of demand from both work and PhD was at times almost intolerable, but I felt I had to finish, and that desire came before any feelings about whether it was a good experience or a bad one; it was what it was.

While science students in lab teams are traditionally seen as well supported, these can themselves bring other problems, as one student illustrated:

> It was good overall. I learned an awful lot about myself in terms of abilities, laziness, determination and self-belief. It was good in that I really challenged and amazed myself at what I had achieved, and what I could achieve if I put my mind to it . . . The bad things were that sometimes we were treated very badly, facilities were poor and often we were seen as cheap labour for the department. There was very little money so when chemicals were wasted or equipment broke down, there was no money to fix it, so repairs were often homemade and bad.

Developing self-knowledge over time was important to many others in this group, along with other types of knowledge and skills. Completers varied over which times they experienced as good or bad, but writing up did come in for particular comment from science students:

> It was very hard work, long hours (my health was poor for quite a while related to stress), sometimes lonely, but in general I enjoyed the mental and physical challenges. I started a demanding full-time job the day after three years' funding expired – writing up while working full time was not successful and eventually I took three months off to finish it – I did not enjoy this bit!
>
> I had some brilliant times. My fellow students became close friends and there was a lot of camaraderie. The practical aspects were good, but writing up was a horrible experience. People try and warn you what it is like, but I don't think anything could have prepared me for the isolation and the hard slog it turned out to be.

While intellectual challenge tended to be a focus for positive comments, the 'student experience' often was not. One social science student spelt out clearly that the experience varied hugely according to where she was – beginning, upgrading, continuing or finishing. So, for example, she described how interaction with other students was – for her – alarming in the early stages, whereas later she worked well with 'reading groups':

> At the beginning, I felt quite excited about finally doing my PhD. That quickly dissolved into complete insecurity! The departmental seminars and colloquia and reading groups did nothing but highlight my utter lack of knowledge and critical thinking skills. Some (certainly not all) of the other students were very critical – not only of the readings, but of the other students' ideas and work in progress. It was a very difficult dynamic for me.

Her supervisors were a large part of building confidence over time, but not the whole story which included her own growth and development through her own life, through working with reading groups and through tackling her writing issues. She describes ably the ways in which the PhD can be much, much more than an intellectual exercise:

> Now, looking back, I feel like the PhD process was boot camp – getting torn down and rebuilt. That's how it was for me. A very emotional process – going from the depths of feeling completely stupid and undeserving, to looking at a 300-page bound manuscript with my name on it! But, of course, that rebuilding process is always in progress . . . But I also feel liberated by having finished the PhD. I feel so free – to research whatever I want, now, or to even change professions altogether.

I suspect the other respondents would agree with her: bad though it was, there is a pride that comes from knowing you are the kind of person who survived this intellectual boot camp. Like this graduate, completers saw good supervision as an essential ingredient in making progress as PhD students. I had asked a further question: which aspects of supervision did you find effective and which aspects did you find unhelpful?

Supervision

Expectations, on both sides, played a large part in forming the tacit criteria for goodness or badness of supervision. Only two completers found their supervision to be 'good', without qualification, providing what the two felt they had needed most. One of them, a science graduate, said:

> All my supervisors were great. They gave me lots of materials right at the beginning that got me off to a good start and would always respond to any of my questions on the same day or as soon as possible after. They were happy to meet regularly and to give constructive, critical feedback. They made it quite clear what was expected for a PhD.

For many science PhDs, access to materials and equipment is essential, to which this student added responsiveness and getting off to a speedy start. This completer had obviously managed the tricky business of receiving criticism, which he perceived as constructive. A social scientist, too, found supervision to be a constructive experience:

> Supervision helped me 'find my voice', particularly writing and presenting. I truly believe my PhD is mine – the supervision drew it out of me and no one can take that away from me.

These two last two were, however, unusual in this group in being unequivocal, most found supervision to be a mixture of positive and negative experiences, with a few feeling that essential ingredients were missed. Completers' needs were highly individual and supervision was beset by the same mixture of good and bad experiences that can affect any close, working relationship. Personal styles as well as individual expectations of both student and supervisor shaped the supervisory experience, as one science student described:

> Don't get me wrong, at times I did have good supervision, and some very productive meetings. I think things could have been a bit more structured though. It may not be the same for all students, but I think I would have worked better that way. My supervisor was also very good at covering all bases when I finally did get help writing up. I knew that there was no way I would be walking into my viva with gaping holes in my research that could have been picked apart.

This response illustrates a recognition that supervisors' strengths vary according to the stage a student is at in the process. Because it is a relationship, the following response from another social scientist reminds us that the early stages can be beset with the tension of 'newness':

> I found the first few supervision sessions that I had a bit difficult, probably because I hadn't yet decided on my research questions and wasn't quite sure what was expected of me. I didn't really know what a supervision session was supposed to involve.

Supervisors sometimes appeared to have their own, preferred way of supervising which did not always take account of the student in front of them. For two social scientists, their supervision focused substantially on writing. This is a common style of supervision, but not always one that is easy to adjust to. One completer described her discomfort with this as the *only* basis for meetings:

> Also, my supervisors required me to submit written work for every meeting. This was very important for forcing me to articulate ideas in a format that they could then engage with. I wrote way, way, way more than ever went into the final thesis, but their requirement meant that I was always writing – from day one until the day I finished. This was very effective for me . . . Once or twice, I made appointments with them to just talk through some ideas or obstacles. But I wonder if it might have been better to have alternated between 'writing' supervisions and just 'conversation' supervisions.

This required, then, that the student take the initiative in changing procedures. Another described their supervision as 'in the old school': he was encouraged to take time to widen his knowledge and to write from the earliest opportunity:

> I had one supervisor and I believe that I was supervised largely in the old school: I was his pupil. He started me looking at the problem before he referred me to any literature. As I was moving into a new knowledge area, he arranged for me to attend two seminar series in order to widen my understanding and introduce me to new theoretical approaches . . . He was wide and thorough in pointing out areas of possibly relevant literature. We met regularly for the first four years (perhaps every month in the first year and then every two or three months) and he got me writing straight away: each meeting centred on a piece that I had written. Some of these writings became the framework for chapters in the thesis.

While traditions of supervision vary between subject areas, it is more usual these days for a student to be supervised by more than one supervisor whatever the focus of their study, as one scientist explained:

> Having two supervisors was good as well, as there was always someone else with a new perspective on things that could point out the obvious when those close could not see the wood for the trees.

Joint and team supervision brings with it other issues; not least, 'good' and 'bad' can stand as contrasts between supervisors. The supervisor of one science student was famous (which she admits has been useful to her career) and showed little interest in her work in the early stages. His interest changed over time, however, and he picked up on her work as she was finishing, when her obvious success took her to the top of his list:

> . . . in the last few months you were top of the list and he would proofread stuff within 24 hours and see you very regularly, even daily.

Fortunately, his attitude stood in stark contrast to her second supervisor:

> My other supervisor was really nice and approachable and always made time for me, and gave me support and advice. He is still very supportive and I have great affection for him.

In some cases these completers saw the supervisory experience as lacking essential elements, including levels of neglect throughout the time of registration. Lack of specific expertise can be especially damaging to progress and too much time can be wasted thereby, as these scientists explained:

> I had regular meetings with my supervisors to discuss progress and I found these very helpful. On the negative side I found that my supervisors lacked some key areas of expertise in which I could've done with guidance. I experienced some steep learning curves because of this.
>
> I was really energized by the academic debates which I had with my supervisor. However he provided no guidance on overall direction and so did not help me in developing my thesis so for a long time felt that I was floundering in the dark.

People changed over time about how bad they judged the same events to be. For one completer, early exposure to independence as a researcher was experienced as unhelpful at the time, but at this stage looking back it is also seen as a boost to self-confidence:

> My supervisor became ill at the start and was ineffective throughout. However he did always tell me I was great which at the time I thought was unhelpful as I wanted constructive criticism, however in retrospect he probably really helped my self-confidence and I have become a successful independent researcher almost immediately.

However much she now feels that she benefited from the experience, nonetheless there is a sense of frustration at the time wasted.

It was by no means clear that everyone shared the same prototype of what makes a good or bad supervisor. One social scientist, for example, found their reassurance sustained progress in completing the final draft of the thesis:

> I found the reassurance and encouragement that my supervisor gave me particularly helpful. Being reassured that a draft chapter was up to standard gave me the confidence to start on the next one. It was also just nice to be able to talk to someone else about the research.

In contrast, another social scientist illustrated Ahern and Manathunga's contention that students can draw clear boundaries to avoid 'confessing' to their supervisors a lack of specific skills. In this case, tight boundaries allowed the student to avoid presenting herself as unprofessional, so discussing only the emotions related to academic work was seen as an important principle for managing supervision:

> I really can't say there were any aspects of my supervision that were 'unhelpful'. At times, I may have liked or needed more emotional support – more acknowledgement of how stupid I was feeling and whether that was normal – but in another sense, I wanted to maintain a professional persona with my supervisors. So I didn't always let them in on my deeper feelings of insecurity. Though I certainly expressed my intellectual frustrations quite a bit to them! I'm also not sure that a supervisor should also be an emotional counsellor. In fact, I think that part of my success was down to this division that I tried to maintain in addressing my supervisors and work through a very professional lens and then setting up other forms of support, like my peer group, friends, for the emotional aspects.

This emotional-intellectual divide echoes Devenish *et al.*'s account, in which control of support remains in the hands of the student. These 'hidden' elements in the jigsaw may include study and reading groups, university counsellors or language and learning support staff and non-departmental courses and groups.

Expectations of supervision were partially rooted in circumstances: for example, part-time students in full-time employment with responsibility for families plus geographically distant from universities broadly experienced differences in supervisory relationships to those who were full-time students with funding and resident at their chosen university. Being a colleague (either in the same or a different university) can shape relationships with supervisors in manifold ways. For example, one social scientist said:

> Supervision meetings, especially with second supervisor, often felt we spent more time talking about their 'current concerns' in part that was my fault for asking,

> and perhaps not 'hassling' for more regular feedback/meetings, however the
> context, my personality, their obvious (or my perception) work overload – meant
> I didn't seem to have support others appeared to have.

In this case, the student was already in collegial relationships with supervisors that included her awareness of their work needs as well as her own. Certainly, his competence as a colleague appears to have put him at the bottom of the list in terms of needing support for the PhD.

Change

Completers experienced a variety of changes over time, in both themselves and their supervisors. One message that came through clearly from this group was that supervision changed: it changed in style over time, there were changes of supervisors, circumstances changed due to supervisors' illnesses and changes of job and institutions. In addition to changing jobs, supervisors travel – some for long periods of time, as this next response shows us. One student was persuaded to change her PhD topic due to changes in both her and her supervisors' circumstances (although she later regretted taking this advice). In this instance, the social science student's changes appeared to coincide with that of the supervisor's post-sabbatical interests:

> When my supervisor returned, he persuaded me to take up a new PhD on the
> grounds that the new topic was my current interest and that I already had the
> data; this turned out not to be the case, and so I changed from a topic for which
> I had all the data, to one for which I had to collect data. This made my work much
> more difficult.

Whatever had made this seem a reasonable decision soon evaporated, leaving the student with more data collection and adding on a few extra years of part-time study.

One social scientist lost two supervisors who suited him exceptionally well, for two who suited him much less:

> My first two supervisors motivated me, encouraged me and challenged my
> intellect in a very positive way. They also made me feel they were mentoring me
> into a profession. The model of how it should be I guess. But when they both left,
> I felt very exposed and unsupported. My later supervisors probably did their job
> properly, they read work, gave feedback, sorted out the formal procedures,
> directed me to the appropriate materials and services, but they had no commit-
> ment to my work, or to me, and they were not really engaged in supporting me
> in the university, beyond the role of 'teacher'.

This echoes Whitelock *et al.*'s contention that a trusting relationship with supervisors promotes creativity (see p. 150) and a creative dialogue, which appeared to be absent in this completer's relationships with the second set of supervisors. Such a contrast made the second two seem inadequate even though he recognized that they could be seen as doing the job sufficiently well.

However, another social scientist described an entirely different set of outcomes when her supervisor moved to another university:

> When my supervisor moved institutions and was awarded a chair (another outcome of taking so long to work through and write up the thesis), his responsibilities increased considerably and he was less contactable. He did, however, meet when I requested. To his credit, he was very flexible with these meetings and we tended to meet halfway between his institution and my own (a distance of about 90 miles). He was also very good, thorough, copious, and considered in his feedback on chapters that I wrote and sent to him, but his turnaround time tended to be long and so I had to find new energy to respond to them.

In spite of the difficulties, including travel and supervisor's increase in duties, it was clear that this student received highly attentive supervision.

'Blended learning' represents a relatively newer set of options available to supervisors whose students live at a distance: multi-media strategies to take research forward without meeting face-to-face have been made more possible through Skype telephone calls, email and blogs (sometimes known in education circles as 'learning logs'). While supplementing traditional approaches, de Beer and Mason (2009) have described one project for making blended learning a systematic basis for their PhD programme as a means to manage increased numbers of student registrations in situations where resources for supervision have not been increased equivalently. Certainly, these approaches could revolutionize managing study at a distance and supervisor absence.

Implications for supervision

- To understand what makes completing a PhD possible, supervisors need to take seriously the institutional, national and international pressures that constitute the students' framework for study. But as well as making sense of the 'completion jigsaw', completion needs to be understood as a key stage in an experiential, educational process that requires a sizeable step up in students' energy and commitment. There is change in mindset required, from the ambivalence described by Ahern and Manathunga and Styles and Radloff, to seeing successful completion as a real option, which is made more possible by a constructive, planned research education but can, nonetheless, still be achieved in unpromising circumstances. Understanding and awareness on the part of supervisors was reported as an important element in achieving successful completion.

- Students come in all shapes and sizes. Some are full-time, fully funded students resident at their place of study. Many are part time, in full-time employment with demanding lives and visit their university only occasionally. People who have studied full-time in the past may combine completion with starting new lives and new jobs. Awareness of these multiple pressures form a part of the sensitive supervisor's repertoire in supporting successful research.

- Supervisors and students both arrive at supervision with a variety of different and, on occasions, mutually exclusive sets of expectations and understandings about each others' roles and responsibilities. It is a relationship, so suffers from all the problems that come with setting up any new, working relationship. It works better at some times than it does at others. Joint supervision or supervisory teams can offset personal differences and balance out skills and characteristics, providing safety nets for when supervisors move institutions. But supervisory teams intensify the social sophistication needed on both sides: students, for example, are likely to need social skills that enable them to manage a team of supervisors. Similarly, supervisors need to work cooperatively and constructively with fellow supervisors, providing an interesting challenge for colleagues working in a highly competitive environment.

- A cartoon image of universities is one that portrays static populations, in which research students study with one master who has taken root in a cloistered college. In reality, universities house transient populations with changes taking place all the time. For research students, they themselves change significantly in relation to their research and their supervisors, expectations will change, lives move on. Supervisors move between institutions, become ill and take sabbaticals. Reviewing progress constructively includes the capacity to reflect on how all parties are handling the many, sometimes subtle and sometimes seismic, shifts in circumstances.

- Such transience means that supervisors cannot depend solely on meetings in their own offices for supervision sessions to take place with completing students. Increasingly, supervisors need to transfer the multi-media skills they have developed on taught courses to the practice of supervision. Members of this group were supervised by email, via Skype and video conferencing, as well as by the traditional meeting face-to-face in a university office. The question of what style of relationship exists between supervisor and student is shaped as much by these factors of physical conditions as they are by personal preference and tradition.

- Successful doctoral education requires space for the 'hidden' ingredients in establishing research communities that support students' intellectual development. This goes beyond providing facilities at university campuses, although dedicated buildings, rooms, offices, staff-student spaces and equipment are important ingredients. In addition, departments, schools and faculties can foster joint group meetings, study and reading groups and online seminars or conversations. Recognition is needed, too, for the benefits of departmental conferences, research training and centrally provided courses and support units.

Implications for supervision—Cont'd

- The capacity of these students to achieve success in their PhDs does not excuse poor or neglectful supervision, but it does raise questions about how the final stages of a PhD are managed. Successful writing-up will depend on what has gone before, yet also requires additional intensity in teaching. While some PhD experiences may be narrated as bad, seeing completion as a separate stage which requires a different mindset allows one to question whether these experiences automatically prevent completion or whether active attempts to build on the positives of the experience can contribute to completion.

Completers reported both good and bad experiences and, rather than hindsight softening memories of the bad, accounts of completion adopted an heroic tone – reflecting a sense of having completed an educational experience that was extraordinarily difficult. Awareness of the heroic nature of the PhD narrative was reflected in the later student and the supervisor surveys, where the themes of the persistence and the personal qualities needed for successful completion were overwhelmingly recognized as relevant.

With the benefit of hindsight, part-time students expressed disappointment with the 'student' part of the experience, while work and family commitments ranked high on their priority lists. There was a wider question about the extent to which students managed the isolation of research and whether or not they felt welcomed into an academic community. In terms of academic dispositions, the independence and solitary endeavour that is the working life of many academics may be experienced by students currently studying for PhDs as disappointed expectations and a lack of care.

Current Students: Making Progress and Experiencing Supervision

4

Chapter Outline

A survey of current students provided insight into how they viewed their experience of the PhD and supervision. Like the completers in Chapter 3, they provided highly personalized, individualized accounts of their pathways through the PhD. But patterns emerged ('family resemblances'), not least a wish to feel welcomed into an academic community. This chapter explores current students' expectations of supervision; what seemed to make progress possible for them and what hampered progress so far; and how they have experienced supervision.

As we have seen in Chapter 3, whatever research funding bodies, governments and universities decide, successful completers described the PhD as an individual, personalized achievement. Current students provided me with similarly personalized narratives about their preferences and expectations, which were situated in specific research contexts. Doing a PhD is an opportunity to focus on a subject matter close to a student's heart, their intellectual interest, obsession or mere curiosity. For those who enjoy scholarship and research, the PhD encourages perfectionism, accuracy, analytical and evaluative thinking, skills in data collection and in academic writing. These attributes are expressed within academic societies that require high-level social skills and behaviours that I have termed 'academic dispositions'.

There are 'family resemblances' in how students describe their experiences. So, for example, in student workshops I have asked the question: what words would you associate with the good aspects of doing a PhD, and which with the bad aspects? The answers are unsurprising and the list of 'good' is long and varied, but the strength of emotion surrounding the 'bad' never fails to shock me. The good include: independence, excitement, satisfaction, achievement, developing, changing, new skills, learning, involvement with other students, contact with good academics, feeling challenged and improved writing. The bad can include: frustration, isolation, disappointment, anger, obsession, feeling lost, unconfident and unsure about completing. The ferocity with which 'the bad' is experienced can lead one to assume that the problems faced are exceptional (which, of course, they may be).

However, Kiley (2009) and Trafford and Leshem (2009) have recently borrowed Meyer and Land's (2006) notion of 'threshold concepts' to describe the uncomfortable experience of negotiating key stages of learning, in this case, to proceed to 'doctorateness'. Wisker and Robinson (2009), too, have recently written on incorporating the need to support students' crossing conceptual thresholds into supervisory practice. The transformational nature of negotiating educational challenge is encompassed in this approach, along with a vocabulary for understanding the PhD as an educational process within which states of transition in passing through 'portals' to new levels and states of understanding is, of itself, an intense, emotional experience. As an approach, it carries with it the danger of interpreting all supervisory teaching as addressing 'stuckness', but it does allow a framework for making sense of intense emotion in students' 'down' periods.

Accepting the normality of intense emotion attached to the developmental challenges of the PhD holds the potential to make it harder to recognize at the time what is an expected period of 'downness' and what is a severe problem that requires action or support. Unlike successful PhD graduates, current students are not in a position to assess whether or not challenges faced are going to stop them from completing. The PhD is a work in progress, a state of permanent transition, as a piece of writing, as research and as a part of life. The few students who give the impression that they can genuinely visualize their research project as completed PhDs stand out as exceptions. Rather, the PhD seems to be foggy in the minds of students – an everlasting commitment to a project that appears to have no end. Hence, I checked out via a survey what current students saw as enabling them to make progress and what they thought got in the way, as well as asking about their perceptions of supervision.

Students are increasingly used to being surveyed for feedback on teaching and the experience of being taught (see, for example, Heath, 2002, and Kulej & Wells, 2009). Postgraduate students in the UK have the opportunity to contribute to the Postgraduate Research Experience Survey (PRES), and students from 82 higher education institutions took part in the 2009 survey (Kulej and Wells). My survey, by comparison with Heath's Queensland survey and with PRES, was opportunistic (and so, once again, represents no one institution or particular populations). 114 questionnaires were received from current students in UK institutions in 2007–8:

- 60 per cent were female
- 47 per cent were social science and humanities students
- 20 per cent studied management-related subjects
- 33 per cent were natural science and technology students
- 96 per cent intended to complete a PhD
- 74 per cent were native speakers of English
- 72 per cent were registered full time
- 55 per cent had external funding (over half of whom had research council funding).

In addition to providing responses to 50 attitudinal items assessed by Likert scales, students added detailed comments in response to five open-ended questions. Some strong 'family resemblances' emerged, so I have chosen to describe these using plain percentages.

Overall, they did feel that they were gaining from the PhD experience:

- 81 per cent agreed that their research skills had improved
- 68 per cent felt they had improved as academic writers
- 50 per cent said they had developed their teaching ability.

Work was proceeding relatively smoothly for over half: 56 per cent agreed that they work steadily, and 53 per cent that they regularly experience a sense of satisfaction. Experientially and emotionally, 52 per cent felt part of an academic community, but 64 per cent often felt isolated; 44 per cent agreed that they often felt incompetent, and 35 per cent felt they had lost confidence since starting the PhD. 77 per cent agreed that they 'regularly experience emotional highs and lows'. One respondent succinctly summarized the roller-coaster experience:

> I have found that my feelings have changed considerably over the time that I have been studying. I feel I have been through a well-documented path of highs and lows throughout the four years I have been studying. From talking to other students and lecturers I have found that I seem to have fitted into a similar pattern to everybody else. At one stage of my PhD I very strongly felt as if I had lost confidence, but with some careful encouragement and hard work I have regained much of it and I am probably more confident now than I have been previously.

In this student's case, supportive supervision and encouragement from friends and colleagues was on hand to make progress possible and to help overcome challenges. In what follows, I (1) explore respondents' views of what makes progress possible; (2) examine what hampered progress; (3) analyse views of supervision, including expectations and good, mixed and bad experiences; and (4) I explored the data further to see what, if any, relationship gender and discipline of study have to students' responses.

Making progress

Like the completers that we have seen already (and as we will see later with supervisors) current students accepted a personalized narrative of success and saw their internal, personal characteristics as highly important in determining success.

Table 4.1 What makes successful completion possible?

Successful completion of my thesis will be made possible because of . . .	% agreed
My persistence	96%
My capacity to work independently	88%
My resilient nature	79%
Good supervision	72%
Having a supportive family	64%
Having funding	60%
The right equipment has been provided	48%
Attending research training classes	28%
Having paid teaching work	25%

The advantage of the view that internal characteristics shape outcome is that it leaves control of the process in the hands of the individual student. High self-efficacy beliefs (i.e. what I do impacts on the outcome) are motivating in the sense that continued work on a problem seems worth the effort, even in the face of setbacks. The danger inherent in the view that individual student characteristics determine eventual success is that there are few others to blame, potentially increasing the pressure when hitting an emotional low or when doubting one's capabilities.

Each PhD cuts a highly personalized route through aspects of an existing disciplinary field (or across fields), bringing personal and intellectual development together. There is no one factor alone that ensures progress, rather a combination of meeting (or not) highly individual sets of needs. As one student said, making progress requires:

> Emotional support from a range of sources; constructive criticism of review panel members; informal intellectual support of other departmental staff; appointment of the right external and internal examiners; knowing my PhD problems are 'normal'.

The only external support that (nearly) received the levels of uncomplicated agreement seen for internal characteristics was supervision: 72 per cent agreed that *good supervision* would make successful completion possible, a trend reflected by completers (see Chapter 3) and supervisors (see Chapter 6). It lay, however, below key personal characteristics on the students' list. As one student wrote: *'In the end, motivation is always personal.'* Another commented:

> Generally I have experienced very good supervision, but I have had times when it has been awful. Fortunately those times have been very few and have been outweighed by all the good supervision . . . However I feel that it is a partnership between the two of us and I do have a responsibility to carry out my part in it, rather than be a passive receiver of supervision.

Students, then, can put great pressure on themselves.

Presumably, for the 48 per cent who needed the right equipment for their PhDs, this would have constituted an absolute requirement rather than an optional preference. In contrast, only 28 per cent saw research training courses as relevant to making progress. One student explained how the focus on the detail of their individual project influenced why it was that training was not valued:

> At the high level of specificity in the research work we do, not even 1-to-1 training courses can help . . . I mention 1-to-1 because I don't think there will be such a coincidence that two PhDs at the same institution can benefit from the same training.

The highly specific nature of individual research projects remains at the centre of student accounts. Focus on the subject matter is what makes sense of the experience, even though people share common themes.

What hampers progress?

Personal narratives went beyond seeing individual characteristics as key to success. Barriers that might, logically, be seen by others as hindering progress were interpreted as absolute or relative according to the circumstances of the research, individuals' variety in responding to challenges and the personal preferences of the student. While there was agreement over what supports progress, there was less clarity over what hinders progress.

Table 4.2 What has hampered progress so far?

What has hampered progress so far?	% Agreed
Work commitments	45%
Personal problems	40%
Poor supervision	28%
Poor facilities and resources	26%
Teaching	25%
Lack of funds – money problems	25%

Poor facilities and resources included, for these students, not having access to essential data. While this may not be a widespread problem, when it occurs it can be an absolute problem that prevents (at least temporarily) translating an idea into a real research project. If they cannot either set up experiments or access essential data, science students are particularly vulnerable as this student illustrates:

> My progress was hampered quite considerably in my second year by a catastrophic problem with the experiment . . . I couldn't get any data because we couldn't run the experiment.

And some work can only take the time it takes, no matter how dedicated the student, as another science student said: '*Working with organisms, I am constantly waiting for them to grow so I can use tissue . . . It is not possible to make something grow faster than it is doing.*'

In practical terms, funding from research councils, governments, families and charities makes PhD research possible (particularly full time); fees, accommodation and carrying out the work are expensive items, and need to be paid for over at least four years. Yet interestingly, while 55 per cent of this group had external funding, only 25 per cent felt that funding issues were hampering progress. Lack of funding might be seen, logically, to be an absolute condition that hampers or supports progress, nonetheless there was personal variation in how people framed similar situations. For some, lack of funds was presented as a problem, for others it was presented as an advantage. The general belief that funding allows students to work without distraction was summarized as: 'So that I don't have to undertake paid work and can concentrate uninterrupted.' Yet, another student argued, there is freedom in finding one's own funds:

> I've always had very poor funding, but this has granted me the liberty to do the research in what I really like. Besides, being so poor has been a stimulus to finish quickly.

So, money and funding has a variety of impacts on PGR study. One student made it plain that while they needed to do paid work to provide funding, this was not a problem: 'I do not feel that my progress has been hampered in any way despite work commitments.' Another, however, felt that earning money impacts on time, which in turn affects the quality of work: 'Teaching took a lot of time and I needed that little money because I did not have funding.'

So interpretation of supposed barriers as absolute or relative, inhibiting or liberating, is both personalized as well as highly specific. There was more unanimity about the importance of supervision, with 72 per cent agreeing that 'good supervision was part of what made progress possible'. What, then, were the respondents' expectations and feelings about supervision?

Expectations of supervision: communities and research cultures

Much of what are described as good and bad experiences, mixed and clear criticisms, are based on spoken and unspoken expectations of supervision and the doctoral experience.

> It's not what I expected! Being productive within the timeframe and in order to produce the required wordage means I sometimes wonder if I have been as thorough as I need to be at this level . . . though I do feel I am gaining in knowledge and understanding of my subject to greater depth.

While not necessarily expecting friendship, there was some expectation of being welcomed into an academic community by and through the gatekeeping function of supervision. Survey responses showed that high numbers of students wanted collaboration, careers advice and joint publication.

Table 4.3 What supervisors should be

In the light of your experience supervisors should:	% Agreed	% Disagreed	% neither agree/disagree
Work collaboratively with students	85%	5 %	10 %
Provide career advice	70%	10 %	17 %
Publish jointly with students	63%	6 %	31 %
Provide emotional support	49 %	20 %	30 %
Become friends with students	44 %	19 %	36 %
Offer guidance only about research	24 %	49 %	26 %

The notion of supervisors providing emotional support is as much about (1) students wanting supervisors to engage more fully with their experience as (2) wanting involvement in academic communities, offsetting isolation and over-dependence on supervisors.

> I think that it is not necessary (or possible) for a supervisor to provide general emotional support, but it is crucial that the supervisor understands the emotional aspects of doing a PhD, be sensitive to those aspects, and at the very least try not to be harmful to the student in this regard.

Another student spelt out the kind of interest s/he had hoped for on the supervisor's part:

> I expected my supervisor to help me a lot more in many ways, such as helping me to find funding, conferences and job opportunities in the field. Joint publication would be great . . . Generally I wanted him to take more of an interest in my work and progress: I need motivating and supporting . . .

The feeling that supervisors are not really interested, have students imposed on them or are only concerned with fully funded students arose. A notion of being 'professionally pleasant' was mentioned:

> If supervisors become friends with students, it is nice, but it is unreasonable to expect this as a part of the job. They should, however, at the very least be

> professionally pleasant . . . Advice on careers from supervisors would be useful, as they know the system better than the careers service itself.

Careers advice in this case refers to academic careers, which only a certain percentage of doctoral students will want. But the idea of a supervisor as a mentor, beyond the PhD itself, at the start of an academic career is still active.

Students' comments about guidance provided additional insight into how the nature of the general research culture in a department or school is perceived to impact on the PGR experience. For some, the expectation of welcome went beyond supervisors' attitudes, looking for a research culture in which their isolation was lessened and through which their work became possible. One described this as: *'Joining an academic community; mutual encouragement within the faculty, department and residence; better peer contact – less oblique criticism of my work; desire to become part of the academic community.'* As one student explained, this is not just a personal preference, but part of succeeding in the work:

> Not being part of the academic community means that . . . it becomes difficult to develop the academic breadth around your field as there is no one to discuss new ideas with.

Where the academic environment feels impoverished, students felt lost and overly dependent on their supervisors:

> Lack of guidance, lack of a social network of other PGR students with whom to exchange about readings, review panels, which seminars to attend, research methods.

Aware of how departmental cultures impact on supervision, one student wrote:

> Lack of a departmental information-and-support structure for PhD students (thus leaving us especially dependent on our supervisors).

However, students' perceptions of the same elements in their academic environment was, again, highly personal. Two, for example, said: *'Not belonging to any academic community'* and the lost, disoriented feeling associated with an extended experience of isolation, *'Don't know where I am.'* Another felt that isolation was not a problem:

> The nature of research means the majority of it must occur in isolation. This in itself is not a problem as long as the direction of study is clearly mapped out for

the individual, regardless of whether they are competent or confident. Supervisors are absolutely vital in ensuring the individual can focus their efforts on what is important for their area of study.

It will vary from discipline to discipline how likely it is that supervisors will be engaged in mapping out the direction of study for the student – in some disciplines this is the students' work. Expectations of being welcomed into an academic community may be less with distance students or those on doctoral programmes, although (as did completers in Chapter 3) they may assume resident students to be a part of a richer community. People drew on their own resources to combat the sense of isolation (friends and fellow students). One student described how good supervision in place of a research community makes the work possible at all:

> As a mature, employed student with a settled family life coming to the end rather than at the beginning of a career, I have enjoyed the experience of being a research student . . . I don't feel that part-time students like me are really integrated into the university . . . it's a 'do it in spite of' situation, and I have been lucky to have such supportive supervisors . . .

Experiencing supervision – overview

- 63 per cent of this group rated their supervision as excellent or good
- 15 per cent rated their overall experience of supervision as poor
- 12 per cent *strongly* agreed that they had experienced poor supervision such that it had hampered progress (28 per cent agreed in total to this item)
- Only 3.5 per cent felt that their supervision sessions were too rare (80 per cent disagreed with this)
- Three-quarters found supervision sessions constructive and collaborative
- 73 per cent found supervision sessions were not formal
- 68 per cent found supervision sessions relaxed and supportive
- 63 per cent found supervision sessions challenging
- 15 per cent experienced supervision as upsetting
- 11 per cent found supervision sessions undermining.

Among those who found supervision to be good, people found sessions personally pleasant as well as academically helpful: *'Helpful, balanced in terms of personal and work issues, friendly and I am guided extremely well'*; *'I worked very closely with my supervisor. I would normally meet him several times in one day, when we would discuss the experiment and progress'*; and *'Generally very positive – so far. I'm about to submit and hope this process will continue favourably.'*

A few commented on the intellectual stimulation of supervisory sessions, which one summarized as: *'I would also add that they provoke the flow of ideas, helping me to get a new perspective on my work and a new and sometimes better angle from which to approach it.'* Another said:

> I have been extremely fortunate with my supervisor who has taken an active interest, lent books, given advice and encouraged me when I was wandering off track.

One commented on how a good relationship meant learning a range of skills

> . . . inspiring, my supervisor has always treated me as a colleague and not a student. I even get to read his manuscripts prior to submission to publication, and we have an article under peer review for publication together, and two more coming.

However, another commented insightfully on how having good supervision was not protection against the difficulties of doing a PhD:

> I've been lucky enough to have a wonderful supervisor, a supporting sponsor and a lot of luck, and still, sometimes doing a PhD was emotionally very hard. I've heard horror stories from friends not having as much luck with their supervisors and it makes the process even harder than it is.

Not all found pleasantness helpful. One criticized her supervisors for not being frightening enough:

> My only criticism of my supervisors would be that they are too understanding and supportive. This may sound strange, but sometimes I have felt that I might have progressed quicker if I had been a bit more scared of going into supervision like some of my colleagues have been.

Not surprisingly, given that 75 per cent found supervision sessions to be generally constructive, many supplementary comments echoed completers' accounts in Chapter 3 and represented mixed accounts, both good and bad. Two competing comments illustrate how different students both experience and require different approaches:

> I always come away from supervision feeling much more positive and very supported. My only criticism is that I would prefer my supervisor to be more critical at times.

In contrast, the second said:

> Excellent training in academic defence. Very thorough. Very demanding. Mini-vivas. Poor in terms of encouragement.

Most students now experience 'joint supervision': rather than one supervisor per student, they work with at least two supervisors. In some institutions, students work with a panel of supervisors, whose chair may need to qualify according to specified criteria (e.g. numbers of recent successes in completion or numbers of PhDs examined recently). One student commented, after changes in supervision within his first year: *'Two supervisors from the start is much safer.'* However, joint supervision brings its own challenges for students trying to build up trust and to find some certainty: *'Conflict between all three supervisors, trying to pull me in different directions to suit their own ends.'*

Fourteen students strongly agreed that poor supervision has hampered their progress. I decided to look at this group in greater detail: eight women and six men, five were registered in social science subjects, five in science and four in arts subjects. Six had awards from funding councils and eight were currently full-time students, although some of the six part-timers had previously registered full time. The Mann-Whitney test (see Sheskin, 2004) was used to compare this group with the rest of the respondents, to see if there were any significant differences in responses on the Likert items; and the mean responses were used to estimate the direction of shift for those items that appeared to be significant. Those significant at the 5 per cent level are reported here.

The group of 14 were *more* likely to agree that lack of funds and resources had hampered progress; that supervision is undermining, frustrating, rare, upsetting and poor or very poor. They were more likely to agree with these statements:

- I often feel incompetent
- I have lost confidence since I started
- I often feel isolated.

The group were less likely than the rest to agree that success is made possible by the right equipment, research training and funding. They were less likely to agree that supervision is constructive, collaborative, relaxed or supportive. They were also less likely to agree with the following statements:

- I work steadily
- My IT skills have improved
- I feel part of an academic community.

Among the seven who added comments, accounts of 'bad' were as highly personalized as those of good and mixed. Five found the working environment uncomfortable: fitting into departments, the internal politics, and the loneliness of being attached to a supervisor who appeared not to care. Egan *et al.* (2009) emphasized the importance to student satisfaction of supervisor's time regardless of subject area. Whereas, for these dissatisfied students, time and access to supervision was linked to supervisors' attitudes – perceived by their students as appearing not to care. One self-funded student felt there were systemic reasons for lack of concern:

> . . . it is very frustrating to feel that staff are more interested in the funded students, who in my view need less support not more . . . it feels very unjust. I was also given a second supervisor who was, similarly, academically excellent but not very available.

A student described the impact of supervisors who appear not to be interested in the student or their project:

> A disinterested lecturer in a classroom setting can make it harder to learn, but in itself is not the end of the world for a student (at least if it's not that way with every lecturer). A disinterested supervisor, however, can have devastating implications for a research student. There needs to be some guarantee for the student that their supervisor has both the desire and the ability to supervise.

The system itself did not make sense and did not feel fair: struggling to establish research aims, managing review panels (described by one as a 'significant distraction from research'). Another student described their department's approach to review panels as bureaucratic and wanted them to become more useful for students. Paradoxically, this chimes with the supervisor central to Cribb and Gewirtz's (2006) case study who argues that supervision has become part of a machine for processing PhDs and that progression monitoring, an aspect of the bureaucratization of supervision, means that various 'threats hang over the student's head all the time' (p. 226).

One described the process as battling but waiting 'for the whole thing to be over'. Another deeply frustrated student was reminiscent of Rudd in commenting that PhD students cannot voice their concerns, rather they have 'to wait for the day when all people whom we may bruise with our comments have not got any more power on our future careers'. Starting the PhD as a high-flier, this student was finding the process undermining and experienced the work environment and lack of future job prospects in academe demoralising and dispiriting. Another commented:

> What is lacking is a way in which complaints can be made in absolute secrecy about your supervisor(s) without the chance that the parties involved ever get to know. I have been thinking about this but do not have a solution.

Negative emotions were listed: bewilderment, frustration, disappointed, marginalized, angry, tired, unsupported, powerless, unappreciated, alienated, feeling a fraud, neglected, isolated. One student had changed supervisors, but found that feelings of guilt and anxiety persisted, even though the situation had improved. This group depended on 'hidden' supports: friends, families, fellow students and support services available to them in universities. A survey, of necessity, is a snapshot of a moment in time, and it would take longitudinal work to assess if these responses represent an unreconciled crisis in students' work or represent, finally, the whole of their experience.

If borrowing from 'threshold concepts' (see Kiley, Trafford and Leshem, and Wisker and Robinson, 2009), one might argue that the crossings inherent in doctoral education are inherently uncomfortable and that transitional, threshold periods are more intensely experienced where the context is perceived as generally unsupportive. Yet, within this framework, the greatest risk for doctoral students is not achieving change and completing transition through developmental stages. One danger as a trainer is to provide highly coloured case studies for discussion, as a means of trying to get course participants to engage with how it feels on occasions to be a PGR student. However, this can overlook the potential impact of 'mundane' frustrations resulting from the key developments needed to achieve doctoral status and the misunderstandings and differences in viewpoints that are commonplace in designing and carrying out research projects. Further, mundane misunderstandings and key areas of development can be made more or less disastrous by what else is happening in students' and supervisors' lives and how the challenges of the mundane are managed by supervisors. The following scenarios represent the complications arising from mundane and common occurrences rather than dramatic events.

Scenarios: good, bad and mixed

Alex has experienced frustration since arriving to do a science PhD. Alex had intended to study with X – a major name in the field. While X is one of a panel of three supervisors, the other two supervisors hold no interest for Alex. Further, at a recent workshop Alex had been shocked to hear that success in the viva depended on an external examiner (as yet unknown) and not dependent on supervisors' judgements. While Alex finds supervisors two and three pleasant, they are less experienced than X and their subject areas are related but different. Alex meets them separately, and is frustrated that they give different advice and say that Alex must sift advice and take responsibility for decisions. It is not clear to Alex how to take these decisions and who feels that all the supervisors are evading responsibility.

Jay is a gregarious and humorous Social Science student, funded by a two-year university studentship. After being registered for two years as a full-time student, an ill parent led Jay to intercalate for a year. Returning to study as a part-time student, Jay took administrative and teaching jobs at the home university and a neighbouring one. Jay is an active character and has collected large amounts of qualitative and quantitative data. Jay has been writing steadily, but is completely frustrated by the supervisory panel's focus on theory and theoretical frameworks. They cannot seem to agree between themselves what is a suitable theoretical framework for Jay's study. Jay, privately, considers the subject to be an applied one and is bored by theoretical discussions.

Chris had started a PhD with high hopes of becoming an academic in an arts subject, but had become increasingly unfocused and unsure as time had gone past. Attendance at conferences and involvement in departmental teaching has made Chris less comfortable with the way academics conduct arguments and discussions, the competitive environment and the pickiness over accuracy and detail. The isolated nature of university work and stressful interactions with colleagues seem to be accompanied by endless training for teaching, for research, for 'transferable skills'. Chris was finding supervision sessions increasingly hard to manage. It was not that the supervisory panel were unpleasant, just that the relentless cycle of writing and receiving criticism had made Chris feel that academic achievement was impossible.

Gender and discipline

Personalized accounts are shaped by students' prior experience and socialization in the world, which in turn interacts with the demands of the context in which they work and live. So, I wanted to know if two factors (gender and discipline) which are generally considered to shape experience of postgraduate life were impacting on responses to my survey. I took the simple route of comparing the distribution of significant means of responses on the 50 attitude items in my questionnaire, using non-parametric statistical tests. The Mann-Whitney and Kruskal-Wallis tests (see Sheskin, 2004) were used to compare responses, taking significance at the 5 per cent level. Few differences appeared, but those that did are worth closer examination.

Gender

Women students were slightly more likely than men to agree or strongly agree that: (1) personal problems had hampered progress; (2) they sometimes feel incapable; and (3) that supervisors should provide emotional support. The differences were not great and what lies behind this cannot be answered by this data set. It would lend itself to an up-to-date qualitative study to explore what women students' ideals for supervisory relationships look like, conceptualizations of confidence and competence (plus, how these relate to the behaviours associated with 'academic dispositions') and the nature of the problems women students experience and how these shape the doctoral experience. However, rather than solely looking at women, understanding of this phenomenon requires deeper awareness of the social constructs within universities. So, Leonard's book (2001), *A Woman's Guide to Doctoral Studies*, is based on her recognition of the gendered nature of universities. But rather than taking a view of discriminatory practices common in the 1970s and 1980s, Leonard approaches the ways in which universities privilege men (and the middle classes) from an inequality perspective that recognizes the gendered nature of social practices (see pp. 4–8). This requires more sophistication in analysing what Leonard calls the 'micropolitics' of universities and the ways in which gender are relevant.

So, for example, Hunt (2001) has given some insight into how one critical incident surrounding feedback from her supervisor caused her to abandon her studies for a year. She describes her response to the supervisor's nine written comments (which she experienced as 'scathing', p. 358) on her 17,000 words of a 'world-view' chapter as 'gendered' and was experienced by her as a 'sudden and unexpected total demolition of what I had written' (p. 359). Up until that point, feedback had been restrained, but then, up until that point, the changing nature of her own belief system had not been fully expressed. She experienced this interchange as meaning that 'the articulation of a personal belief system' was not acceptable in academe. In what way does she perceive this response to be gendered?

> . . . with the benefit of hindsight, I can see all sorts of ways in which I could, and perhaps should, have responded. In the event, however, I responded from what I would now identify as a very gendered position. I allowed a senior, respected and male colleague to cut across a new identity that I was attempting to forge as full-time academic after many years of part-time work and childcare. (p. 360)

It is disappointing that feedback on a large piece of writing, and one that was clearly significant in the student's development, should have been given in writing and not as part of a more creative dialogue albeit one that encompasses challenge (see, for example, Wisker *et al.* and Whitelock *et al.*). In some ways, this episode can be interpreted as the supervisor's abandonment of his previous collegial behaviour when faced with the need to move into critical mode, illustrating the complexity of such movements between modes. The episode tapped into Hunt's feelings of 'intellectual inadequacy' and regaining a sense of the legitimacy took time (and 'hidden' support from people other than her supervisor). She now sees her 17,000 words differently:

> I can now accept that, perhaps like a dandelion that appears in a carefully tended lawn, the material was not intrinsically 'inferior', but merely presented in the wrong place at the wrong time. (p. 359)

Disciplinary context

Academic context provides a cultural framework in which judgements are made about what is a dandelion and what is not and subject disciplines are key to understanding research cultures. We also know from the history of completion rates for research council funded students that there is a history of relatively more timely completion for science students. Wright and Cochrane's (2000) study indicated that this pattern works at local level as well as national level. Their study of 3,579 students at one civic university between 1984 and 1993 showed that successful completions within four years were likely to be achieved by science-based, research-council funded students (also, international, part-time and with a good first degree). In looking to see if broad disciplinary area (arts, social science and science) related to student responses within my survey, I again compared the distribution of means of responses on each item, through which a limited number of areas of disciplinary difference emerged. All make sense given what is known (in broad terms) about different working patterns associated with areas of study, yet these variations did not fundamentally alter the 'family resemblances' between students in their perceptions of the PhD experience.

1. Social science and science students were more likely than others to agree that they have improved their research skills, although science students were most likely to agree that they had improved their IT skills.
2. All agreed that their persistence would make success possible, but social scientists were most likely to agree.
3. All agreed that their ability to work independently would aid success, but social science and art students were slightly more likely to agree with this. Science students also agreed, but were less likely than the rest to agree, which makes sense where many are working in research teams.
4. Arts students (followed by social science) were most likely to agree that success depends on their resilience and least likely to see success as depending on funding.
5. Whereas, in contrast, science students were most likely to agree that success requires funding, and least likely to see work commitments as potentially hampering progress.
6. Science students were most likely to agree that supervision should include co-publishing where arts students were least likely to agree with this, indicating one of the key cultural differences between these two areas of study.

Implications for supervision

- Current PhD students' narratives reflect highly specific circumstances, because the PhD is about each student's particular focus for research. This shapes students' experiences and is the basis for their relationships with supervisors. In addition, individual needs and preferences as well as expectations about what the PhD is contribute to clarity of communications and misunderstandings that arise. Both students and supervisors can usefully learn to reflect on meetings to learn about how they are working with each other, as well as to consider research progress made.
- Making assumptions about what hampers and what supports progress for each student will probably be misleading – especially what potentially stops an individual making progress. In Chapter 3 we saw that students juggled family, work and changes in circumstances and still produced successful theses. In this chapter, data illustrates how the key issues (including funding) are experienced differently from person to person. What is an absolute barrier for one is a relative difficulty for another, including such basics as funding.

- What is experienced as bad is often not a dramatic case of neglect so much as an accumulation of mundane mismatches and misunderstandings (although occasional matters of outstanding mismanagement may happen). But more often it is a matter of life interfering and people interacting unhelpfully – all within the context of a risky research process within highly personalized needs and specific projects. Mismatches and misunderstandings need not, of themselves, have to lead to disaster. Many can be worked with, but need first to be recognized, acknowledged and reflected upon.
- Supervisors and universities do make tacit assumptions about what knowledge and understanding is needed to make sense of their systems and processes. It is not clear to all new students what successful research is about: how it is executed, how it is embedded in the literature and how these are integrated into persuasive and credible accounts. Where the study is situated within areas where research methods and paradigms are contested, uncertainty can be even greater. It is not always clear to students how experienced researchers who are not subject specialists in their area can be of use to them, and this may require discussion. Part of the purpose of the PhD is to 'become' a researcher in this wider understanding, and there is no reason why these structural elements cannot be discussed en route to becoming an autonomous researcher.

Doctoral education is not a series of tasks to be ticked off a list (although there are practical elements and skills), but an educational, developmental education which brings intense frustration attached to intellectual challenge. The path from starting as a novice to finishing as an independent researcher is strewn with complex decisions, mistakes, intellectual and social challenges. Disagreements between supervisors, or answers to questions that sound something like 'it depends', can be hard for students to understand or tolerate and can set off something akin to panic. It depends: on how confident the students are, how far on in the process they are, how much they can recognize such responses as part of an educational process, and their levels of trust in supervision. Supervisors' disagreements and what sound like woolly answers come on top of a lot of uncertainty to be negotiated in the PhD, not least failing experiments, not getting access to collect data, not solving problems. For some students, supervisory support is needed in learning *how* to approach decision-making in research.

5 Alternative Views

Students and supervisors provide key vantage points from which to make sense of the PhD. But others in universities work with PGR students, and to illustrate how distinct different perspectives can be, this chapter draws on interviews with non-academic professionals within universities and academic managers. The experience of being involved when PGR studies have gone wrong influenced their views: they tended towards discussions of training, systems and processes that support student progression. While called on to mediate supervisory relationships and provide evidence of university performance, these professionals nonetheless expressed only a limited sense of control either over external drivers or the management of supervision and its development. Academic managers were close to non-academic professionals in views, although were more informed about supervisor perspectives.

Others, within an institution but outside the supervisory team, now play an active part in ensuring students' progress, and, as such, form part of the current educational context for PhD study and supervision. However, while supervisors and students are engaged with content, focus of study and epistemology, non-academic staff and academic managers stand back from this detail and so are more likely to emphasize processes and structures that are seen as likely to lead to successful outcomes. While aware of the complex social and power structures that Morley *et al.* discuss (see Introduction), they are not actors in PhDs in the same ways that students and supervisors are. This lends their responses an assumption of rationality concerning doctoral education contrasting with, for example, Grant's (2001) argument that 'clean codes' are not possible within inherently unreasonable practices. Academic managers are likely to be (or have been) supervisors and so show greater awareness of supervisor views and experience.

While supervision is a relationship between one or more members of academic staff and a student, the institution is liable if anything goes wrong according to a range of external agendas. Hence, many within institutions have an interest in the conduct, processes and outcomes of supervision without necessarily being supervisors. In Cribb and Gewirtz's (2006) case study of supervision, the supervisor (Andy) described one of the key changes arising from his faculty's recent 'bundle of regulatory processes' as resulting in:

> . . . a change from feeling it is a personal relationship to feeling it is an institutional relationship in which the supervisor plays one part, and the institution is kind of looking over their shoulder at the supervisor and the student all the time. (p. 226)

Indeed, the people interviewed for this chapter may well represent what Andy experiences as the institution's eyes.

As part of the context that shapes current supervision, how then do these professionals view supervisory practices? I make no assumptions about university structures here. While sometimes I use the shorthand term 'the centre', it is an old-fashioned term used to refer to non-academic professions within universities that may be found in central structures, faculties, schools, divisions, sections or departments. Academic manager refers to roles such as divisional directors, deans, directors of study and similar roles. While central staff and managerial staff may be engaged in talking *about* supervision, rather than the experience of *being* supervisors, this chapter illustrates how awareness of alternative perspectives in universities can help make sense of the relationships subsumed under the umbrella term 'supervision'.

Universities are complex institutions and not, in actuality, always easily divided up into 'academic' and 'non-academic'. Those not employed in academic departments may be administrators, but they can also be teachers (of both staff and students) or student support or advice staff. These roles are additional to information staff found in libraries and information technology centres.

Further, administrative functions, in the old sense of professional support for the management of universities, may now be supplemented by policy-making functions and monitoring an institution's relationship to external requirements and agencies – not least, through quality assurance and enhancement activities. It is commonplace in all these roles to find staff with PhDs; and managing information, through traditional research as well as through data management, has become a key function in non-academic roles in order to analyse one's own institution, but also to relate it to the context of the wider higher education sector. Academic managers may still be teaching, supervising and researching; or they may have left these roles for committees and oversight of an academic section or activity.

This chapter draws on eight interviews with three administrators, one educational developer, one student adviser/counsellor and three academic managers; for most of this group, their work contributes to the wellbeing of both supervisors and research students, hence they tend not to identify overly with either of these two groups. Their responsibilities are a combination of administrators managing day-to-day systems and juggling the impact on institutions of external drivers, such as the QAA code of practice; while providing support and picking up the pieces of PhDs that appear to have gone wrong. They contribute, then, to the overall institutional management of risk and quality assurance processes; supporting the development and implementation of institutional policies; and they contribute to solving problems arising from academic activities, albeit when the main parties involved cannot find solutions between themselves.

Rudd commented in the early 1980s that postgraduates saw little to be gained and much to be lost in complaining, and he suggested that research students needed someone outside their school or department to act as an 'independent arbiter' (p. 122). Externally, the Office of the Independent Adjudicator (OIA) has begun to develop a collection of completed PGR cases and findings that provide an external view of what they judge to constitute reasonable behaviour within universities (see, for example, their 2005 report). The OIA reported on its workshop on mediation and campus ombudsmen and commented, 'It is probable that UK universities have individuals performing a similar role but with different titles, such as Dean or personal tutor' (p. 10, 2005). These are the roles that individuals with management responsibilities and, as we will see in this chapter, at the centre of institutions can on occasions find themselves called upon to play – a vantage point that often requires them to be tuned into the tenor of changes and moods in their wider institution.

It was a student adviser who stated to me clearly that the view of supervision from the centre of an institution was probably skewed: that detailed engagement with PGR students happened for him when the process had gone badly wrong and often when some grievance procedure was about to be started. Other administrators indicated that they knew, anecdotally, that supervision often went reasonably well, but *all* the ones that went so wrong that they required intervention came to their doors (no matter how few in any given year). Echoing Rudd's students, who may still have been hoping to salvage something constructive and so avoided making official complaints, by the time students take grievances to advisers and administrators, they have often lost hope of improving matters within their subject area. Those who feel there is nothing left to lose can be extremely angry people.

Many administrators and managers are tasked with gathering statistics and overseeing procedures that ensure externally driven policies and procedures are in place in their institution (e.g. compiling institutional completion rates). Where, at departmental and subject level, some outside requirements may seem distant and even irrelevant to supervision, for administrators and managers these are the drivers that sit at the heart of quality assurance, quality enhancement and supervision discourses. People in non-academic roles may experience themselves as neither able to control external pressures nor the supervisory practices they are tasked to mediate.

This chapter, then, explores four themes that emerged from these interviews. First, attempting to devise solutions to problems puts such staff in the middle of layers of miscommunication and relationships that have broken down, as we will see in the next section. Second, one favoured strategy for avoiding broken supervisory relationships is 'training' for supervisors; and in what follows we will see that this is often a euphemism for control of completion rates and a means of ensuring a more structured approach to supervision. It is often assumed that academic staff resist development courses, but this common view is challenged by the trainer interviewed. Third, people in central roles were highly aware of the impact of external drivers for change on institutions and this, combined with their involvement in problematic supervisory situations, caused them, fourthly, to be aware of the pros and cons of a variety of models of supervision.

Communication and expectations

Fundamental to many themes emerging from these interviews is an assumption of profound and sometimes contradictory expectations on the part of both students and supervisors. Staff–student relations can appear to sit on a continuum of misunderstanding and, no matter how well the relationships appear to work, seem rooted in tacit expectations on both sides, a view reflected by the student adviser who said that no matter how good the department:

> . . . it doesn't mean that every single PhD student will have their own office, their own computer, they are going to be sharing and it's not going to be a huge corner office with ten windows.

As we saw in Chapter 4, levels of human emotion and misunderstanding can be high around the PhD: where students have invested so much of themselves, feelings are difficult to manage if the degree feels like it is going wrong; and because they see students at times of difficulty, people in central roles often see extreme emotions. One administrator was sympathetic as to why it is students can become highly emotional when the PhD does not appear to be working out successfully:

> . . . it is a disappointment for people who are devoting a huge amount of time and effort, blood, sweat, tears, money – the sacrifices that are involved in so many ways – it doesn't sit well . . . if they have to come to terms with thought that this isn't going to go any further . . .

But even when sympathetic, it can be hard to find a kind way of communicating clearly because of competing expectations and misconceptions about the PhD. The same interviewee said:

> I had bizarre set of exchanges with a woman who had, to all intents and purposes, been told to rewrite and resubmit . . . the simplest way to do this is just to follow the instructions that she has been given, and she's cutting up rough with the supervisor and also about the examiners . . .

She felt that students needed to understand the PhD and prepare for it as an exam like any other and learn to limit unnecessary risks by understanding better what sort of process they had engaged with.

Supervision is riven with differing expectations of what the PhD is; different understandings of the same meetings and of the intent behind instructions, feedback or advice, all of which becomes uncomfortably apparent when the relationship has faltered. Loss of trust on both sides is tied up with beliefs about intellectual capacity and what constitutes academic failure at this level. Does motivation, or the lack of it, count higher than ability?

> The other issue that I have in my mind, I suppose . . . is . . . the difficulty we have with those students who are apparently highly qualified and highly motivated and

then don't get the job done. Many, many years ago a friend of mine said, 'the well organized second-class mind will outperform the disorganized first-class mind every time'.

While not stated as baldly as this, we will see in later chapters how much supervisors share this view that students' personal characteristics, such as persistence or ability to study independently, matter in achieving a successful PhD (a view that coincides with that of the successful completers discussed in Chapter 3 and current students in Chapter 4).

The student adviser explained the difficulties of unravelling and mediating decisions that have been made within student–supervisor relationships in which there is plenty of room for misunderstanding. As is often the case in human relations, two sides can hold completely clear yet contradictory viewpoints. While, on occasions, it could be a straightforward matter for the adviser to decipher events (e.g. where email evidence illustrated the student's grievance clearly), most of the time *'it was almost impossible to get to any real understanding of what actually happened'*. It is easy to forget from within universities how a lack of understanding of the system can turn into painful confusion once trust is lost, as the adviser illustrated when a student took exception to review panel members:

> One of the students that I saw could not believe that the postgraduate review panel was made up of people that weren't in his department because he said 'how can they know?' I said 'it's not an exam board. . .'

In these circumstances, it becomes the role of the adviser to decode and explain the system.

A more common role is to act as advocate, which can mean trying to make some rational sense out of a long-term academic relationship that has gone sour and where the student is deeply attached to their study. To make sense of a failing student– supervisor relationship requires adroit mediation skills, in which a big task for the adviser is,

> . . . to put forward 'this is what the student thinks has happened', strip out all of the emotional stuff, strip out 'all my PhD is involved with this', and . . . go into the meeting and say from the student's perspective 'this was the problem, this was the problem, this was problem' and, of course, the supervisor would say 'that wasn't a problem, *that* was a problem'.

While solutions may not be clear, getting both sides to agree the nature of the problems provides a starting point from which, hopefully, they may progress.

Supervisor training and development

For one administrator, making sense of the relatively recent phenomenon of supervisor training could only be achieved by recognizing the changes and pressures surrounding supervision in recent years. Because of external drivers, he saw the entire culture as having changed to a *'culture of completion'* and *'the idea that the supervisor is leading the student towards successful completion specifically within a certain time frame'*. This culture, then, requires trainers to support supervisors in providing a much more structured, somewhat inflexible, approach:

> . . . what is a priority is making sure that at the very start the student has a working title that will go somewhere, the opportunities for changing that and for starting again and so on are now limited.

Like the supervisor, Andy (in Cribb and Gewirtz's study), these changes were interpreted as bringing educational loss in their wake. The loss involved for this administrator was loss of a certain fluidity and flexibility that once allowed for changes in topic where necessary and had more of a sense of negotiation between student and supervisor. It raises questions, too, about the potential willingness of supervisors to commit time to students who are not progressing according to plan.

Models of joint and team supervision make sense from a central perspective. For example, another administrator thought that the notion of supervisor training would become redundant if the system of PGR education was rethought in favour of one in which: *'. . . there would be a distinction drawn much more ruthlessly between the role of the academic supervisor as provider of specialist advice on intellectual scholarly matters and the apparatus that kept the research students on the straight and narrow, kept them fairly watered, provided for, monitored their progress.'* One of the advantages of such a system would be to unhook students and staff from

> . . . this rather hybrid relationship that supervisors necessarily have, being friend, mentor, academic advisor . . . it would, in effect, be a specialization of labour and you would make people confine themselves to those things about which they knew . . .

Such a model of teaching implies, of course, that the personal is problematic rather than a necessary ingredient in an academic, developmental model of teaching:

> . . . because they were at a distance from the student, you might find them more
> willing to apply that academic rigour that says 'well thank you very for much for
> this, it's not very good is it?' because they know that somebody else is round the
> back with a box of tissues . . .

While this viewpoint favours distancing the personal from the intellectual, it
was political rather than pedagogic reasons that she saw as barriers to this
kind of reconstructed model of PGR education.

Staff attitudes were seen by the student adviser as the major barrier to
training and development activities: '. . . *one of the problems is, "I've been supervising for 30 years, what on earth do you think you are doing?" Or "do you know
anything about this subject, this is the way it has to be supervised"*'. For the
student adviser, the individual, experiential nature of PhDs would mean there
are few pieces of advice that one could give about how to supervise that could
not be contradicted – hence, however helpful, the credibility of a trainer would
be limited:

> I think if you're supervising a PhD, chances are you've done one, and I think any-
> one who's been through an experience and then has to teach it will rely so heavily
> on their own experience that trying to encourage any kind of other behaviour . . .
> you'll always get someone in the room saying, 'well, I tried that and it didn't work'
> . . .

The student adviser reflects two common assumptions: that many staff are
resistant to training, plus the expectation that supervisor courses would be
based on generalized advice to staff on how to conduct supervision. The educational developer interviewed, in contrast, talked about changing attitudes –
over time and between generations. Overall, his impression was: '*I think my
sense is that people are much more open to the notion of developing their practice
in a more explicit way.*' An experienced trainer, he had, in the past, found conflicting attitudes where individual staff expressed anxiety about their teaching
to him privately, but within a culture that publicly insisted everything was fine.
Not only had he found such attitudes were crumbling, but that there was also
a huge generational difference:

> . . . you can see the generational thing because now it seems to me the younger,
> the newer entrants are saying 'yeah fine, I'm willing to take the help you want to
> offer me', whereas older people have been saying, 'hold on!'

He saw this change as accelerating, as more and more staff had been through
some kind of training for teaching, in all probability including some version of

supervisor training. According to this perspective, untrained teaching staff will simply retire over time.

Change: the perceived impact of external drivers

Experienced administrators had observed the various iterations of proposed codes of practice from external agencies and one judged the pressures on their institution against what might have been, given early proposals. Having engaged in the earlier discussions about draft versions of the QAA code, one felt that the eventual code was less painful than it might have been and believed that, had the original been retained, it would have brought about change across the sector by severely limiting who could supervise. Another administrator pointed out that originally the PGR experience had been low on the QAA list of priorities (1999 QAA code), and *'it's only once HEFCE and the research councils have got behind it that people have realised that there are issues here that have to be taken seriously.'* He viewed their concerns as legitimate because of anecdotal reports about the variability of PGR experience, *'because it's tied down so much to the one-to-one relationship with the supervisor, there's been huge variations.'* Yet, however legitimate he allowed their concerns to be, he echoed Grant's discussion of 'clean' systems in his recognition of the inherently idiosyncratic nature of supervisory relationships that resists systematization.

While tasked with monitoring codes locally through quality assurance processes, for example, nonetheless being an administrator or a manager does not mean always agreeing with codes of practice: one administrator saw the QAA code as problematic in attempting to bring about inappropriate changes by stealth:

> If you really applied the QAA code properly, why would you bother to be a super-visor? . . . But again it depends on which discipline you're in . . . Now if we think that the QAA code is actually a stalking horse for making all PhD study in Britain conform to a science model, then maybe the sooner we come to get on with it the better. . .

For this administrator, institutions have few levers for enforcing this sort of change in the outcomes of supervision, seeing staff promotion as one of the few potential routes:

> That if you had N research students and they'd not all finished within a reasonable amount of time or had a good reason why they hadn't, then you can kiss goodbye the prospects of your next promotion, and it is one of the ingredients for promotions exercise.

This view is, of course, predicated on the assumption that staff incentives will automatically filter through and influence student performance, tacitly endorsing the assumption that supervisor behaviour *alone* ensures successful completion.

For the student adviser, however, thinking about a code of practice does not, of itself, ensure quality. One problem being that possible compliance with codes of practice could potentially stop people trying once they have met minimum standards: '*I also think that having a benchmark, it's like saying "right, we're going to get this good and then that's alright we can stop"*.' And, in part, the student adviser viewed the level of prescriptiveness implied by any code of practice (no matter how general) as potentially unsuccessful in ensuring fairness for students:

> In the last one [code of practice], had everything from these really woolly statements like 'assessments have got to be fair', right down to 'it would be expected that they'll have two supervisors'. I mean, I think that it's more important that maybe a PhD student has, if there is one expert in the area, they have one supervisor who is the expert and then have, you might call them a mentor, or some other point of contact, call that a supervisory team if you want to, but don't force a supervisory role on someone who's not interested in that particular topic, because some of them are so specific that you're going to have one person probably in the whole country who knows about it.

While academic managers took a similarly macro view of the impact of drivers for change, theirs was a more detailed view informed by local faculty, school and departmental practices. One interviewee, with responsibility for training within her division, pointed out that supervision is always changing as new supervisors try to work in different ways to their own supervisors. However, in her view that means that there is always a new generation of potentially inflexible teaching habits:

> The bad news is of course, is that they are extremely clear in their own minds how it must be done, and they are very often swinging from one side to the other side. My supervisor treated me in the following way, I hated it, therefore I must treat my students in completely the opposite way, because that is the way I wanted it to be done.

The same interviewee described changes in the PGR student population, *'Fewer British, fewer between the ages of 22 and 25 . . . we have more overseas.'* Professional doctorates, he argued, require considerable technical and practical knowledge on the part of students, *'to be practitioners of some skill and standing in that area'*, and *'that that group of people are a very different prospect to supervise than your 22-year-old who has just got their BA or BSc in something or other.'* She related these changes in the student population, in part, to the changes in the PhD, itself, *'You can argue the profile of the body to be supervised is actually changing in certain ways because of that dynamism of degree structure and one needs to be prepared for that'*. This view was endorsed by another academic manager, who commented that change extended to include an extensive menu of choices available to potential PhDs students: PhDs by publication, work-based doctorates, doctoral programmes and *'even the traditional PhD is a very different animal to what it was, because of external pressures, when we went through the system'*.

Like their administrative colleagues, academic managers regularly described externally driven changes, acknowledging the ways in which supervision has been opened up to the public scrutiny of a range of stakeholders: *'Expectations across the sector, expectations by the government, the Research Councils, employees are all now hitched up very closely towards PGR work. . . .'* However, this macro-level awareness was linked to detailed awareness of academic colleagues' responses. So, one interviewee saw recent changes as ways of enhancing supervision: *'It is not that they're not doing a sound job, but they're not going as far as they might or should. . . .'* Further, he raised the sense of ownership that research supervisors have of the whole process and, rather than displaying a resistance to change, some colleagues display a resulting lack of awareness as to what supervision has to do with others:

> . . . that's my project', 'that's my student', 'I am good at this, leave me alone, I'll get them there', and actually don't engage with the wider issues, and that's a major challenge.

While these academic managers see 'problem cases', they also understood better why some supervisors resisted what can seem like unrealistic systems for managing supervision. Monitoring systems are not perceived as benign, and Cribb and Gewirtz illustrate how supervisors are remodelled to take part in a 'punitive climate characterized by threats and sanctions' (p. 227) towards the students. Hence, one manager raised the problem of putting seemingly bureaucratic policies related to change into practice: policies and advice about 'having a paper trail' that tracks supervision could, he felt, make the relationship more formal in unhelpful ways. Meeting students informally, perhaps in passing in corridors and at seminars, is not accounted for in paper-trail systems. Supervisors found that this more formal approach, he felt, would change relationships for the sake of being prepared for the few cases in which supervision has gone wrong. While current practices are deemed to be necessary for a variety of instrumental and educational reasons, not everyone saw them as ideal and would agree with Cribb and Gewirtz when they argue 'we would not necessarily want to equate the idea of good supervision with current practices' (p. 228).

Models of supervision

From a central perspective, the worst scenarios when they go wrong are those where students and supervisors have been trapped in a tight, highly personalized apprenticeship, a one-to-one relationship that has gone wrong. When it is impossible to track back accurately over what has happened then, being a highly personal relationship, it is hard to find pragmatic ways forward. From this perspective, joint supervision, shared supervision and review procedures appear to be commonsense ways of avoiding what to this group are known and obvious difficulties. So the educational developer described:

> . . . anecdotally where supervision goes the most wrong is where the supervisor–supervisee relationship is a closed one, that there is no fallback, there is nobody else who knows what's happening particularly, and if that person disappears for any reason then the whole thing just falls apart, and that cannot be a good thing.

He was acutely aware that there has to be a 'fallback position' which would include someone holding an official position (e.g. postgraduate convenor of studies, co-supervisor) and that carrying out the role effectively would depend upon power relationships within a department or division:

> There's no point them being the favoured junior person in the department and they're having to deal with inadequacies in the supervisions of the extreme, senior professor who is not about to change any of their practices regardless how many times that the poor supervisee complains or expresses disquiet.

Hence, in this trainer's view, some systemic ways were also needed to support strategies for keeping student–supervisor relationships more open to scrutiny by tightening review processes by *'making sure that is a real process whereby students' progress is evaluated properly'* and that this is matched with *'help and support and guidance'*.

One popular strategy for breaking down the personalized model is joint supervision or the supervisory team. One administrator explained that one of the advantages for both student and supervisor of joint supervision is that it offsets the intensity of one-to-one relationships. But the 'supervisory team' approach is more than an organizational strategy: it is expected to militate against the 'apprentice' model of supervision by breaking down the assumption that every supervisor has to be a world expert on a subject. Hence, these systems attempt to encompass conflicting demands: for example, joint supervision cannot ask for supervision only by those with most expertise in a given topic (in some subjects and departments only one such expert may be available to the student). So, while liking the idea of joint supervision with its potential for multiple sources of support, nonetheless this administrator recognized a central flaw that can get in the way of their success:

> The apprenticeship model kind of implies the master, and that's the problem and, of course, for a successful PhD you do need to be at some point, in touch with somebody who is actually examining a lot . . . I might be a great supervisor with somebody starting but I'm not actually up-to-date with what is a successful PhD in my subject at the moment, whereas somebody who supervises 10, 12 people may not be a very good supervisor but has that kind of knowledge, it's trying to get the student to have all those types of knowledge at different points, but they tend to want to go to the master from the beginning, it's part of the whole apprenticeship model, and I don't know how you get around that.

Getting the 'right' supervisor is, then, unlikely as long as one is looking for one person to oversee the whole PhD from beginning to end and to fulfil all the ideal functions demanded of supervisors throughout the life-cycle of the PhD.

Opening up student–supervisor relationships to other influences is part of ensuring successful completion, which now includes success within a tight timeframe. Hence, discussions about the PhD include rejection of the model of PhD which represented a student's life's work. Rather, the pressure is on to produce something that can be done within three or four years and interviewees were aware that this pressure shapes possible supervisory styles:

> A PhD's a project that should be completed in three to four years, it's about
> producing something of a relevant standard, getting that training as a researcher,
> then being in a position to move on after three or four years into employment of
> whatever type it is, academic, whatever.

Just as joint supervision can be interpreted as more than an administrative
tactic, so imposing tight timeframes can be seen as ensuring a revolution in
some subjects as to what constitutes a PhD.

Perhaps compiling the statistics and answering for an institution's completion rates make administrators and managers highly aware of time and its
potential interactions with supervisory style, and the need to ensure timely
progression. For another interviewee, this means retaining an old-style, robust
approach to managing criticism but, instead, introducing it *earlier* in the
process. He saw this nostalgia for an old-style brutalism as part of developing
the skills needed in the viva long before one reached that stage by learning to
engage with robust criticism.

Academic managers, again, saw the sense in this macro-level analysis
of types of supervision but understood the difficulties at disciplinary level
attached to taking a purely systemic view. One interviewee summarized a
common macro-level view (reaching back to Swinnerton-Dyer and beyond),
that science PGR students have a better experience, while many others are
working in a vulnerable situation:

> . . . it tends to work better in the sciences where the student's part of team, they
> see their supervisor every day because they are working in the lab on the bench
> beside them. There is a good working relationship there and there is good peer
> support . . . The ones I worry most about are the kind of lone scholars, not even
> part time, sometimes full time, working by themselves with sporadic contact with
> the supervisor but otherwise aren't embedded in what's going on . . .

The notion that a science PGR model is the one to be followed by other disciplines is reflected in the debate surrounding the Roberts' report and papers
continue to illustrate ways in which the science model appears preferable: so,
for example, Heath (2002) found that at the University of Queensland science
PGR students 'have more frequent meetings with their supervisors than do
those in the humanities and social sciences, they publish more papers and give
more oral presentations such as seminars' (p. 49). Where science teams are
working well, of course, there is no real need for implementing a 'joint supervision' policy, because there should be a number of supervisory roles. While the

assumption that lab relations are generally good is probably unhelpful to those science students experiencing difficulty, nonetheless a view persists that the three-to-four-year PhD is best suited to certain sorts of science project.

If desirable supervisory arrangements are likely to be embedded in science research teams, they are also seen as an integral part of research activity by others. So, closer knowledge of how colleagues see supervision led one academic manager to comment:

> I think a lot of supervisors would not see supervision as a skill in the way that giving lectures is a skill or even getting research grants is a skill. They would see it as effectively social interaction and not skill . . . they're being nice people or they're being academically rigorous or whatever, but effectively it's personal, it's intuitive . . .

This comment neatly encapsulates the notion of supervisor ownership of research, about which supervisors naturally feel confident and at ease. Hence, supervision is experienced as a personal relationship through which teaching takes place, and has no need of training; whereas the training that is needed is already underway as part of one's development of a subject-specific research identity.

A highly personalized model of supervision makes it easier to explain failings as lying with either student or supervisor and to overlook systemic elements. Reasons, then, for resistance to training or change in supervisory model in experienced colleagues were summarized by one academic manager as being a 'credibility gap' within a personalized model of supervision:

> I think a lot of them would say, 'well, my supervision isn't a problem, my super-vision is fine, I hear horror stories where supervision has gone badly wrong elsewhere . . . so why do I need to be trained for that?'

Implications for supervision

- It is useful for both students and supervisors to become aware of how academic managers and non-academic colleagues are involved in PGR education and recognize the ways in which this shapes opinion. This group saw a need to deconstruct the PhD and make more explicit what the processes are; they recognized how competing sets of expectations and misconceptions can lead to a lack of trust and a breakdown in communications. Involvement in attempts to get two sides with sometimes mutually exclusive viewpoints to recognize and agree the nature of problems leads to concerns about training and management of supervision.

- These interviewees were aware of the implications for supervision of a variety of changes. The impact of strict time limits, of external monitoring and penalties, of the extension of quality assurance measures to include PGR supervision, were all seen as ways of shaping its nature. Measures to open up supervision to public scrutiny were understood as agents of change, but no sense of ownership of or agency in these measures was expressed by this group even if they were viewed by their academic colleagues as instigators of change.
- This group sympathized with supervisors' dilemmas while seeing the limitations of bureaucratic measures intended to bring about change. Training was assumed to be resisted by established staff, but – as the educational developer in particular emphasized – this might be a generational matter, given his observation of changing attitudes. While sympathetic to supervisors' as well as students' perspectives, nonetheless these interviewees were most frustrated at having to pick up the pieces from old-style, one-to-one supervisory relationships in which misunderstanding and miscommunication had built up layers of problems over time.
- While a belief in the efficacy of systems might seem too easy to supervisors, given the lack of engagement in the messiness of subject development, nonetheless supervisors can usefully borrow from this 'systemic' analysis that there are stages common to PhDs in different disciplinary areas that can share similar systems of management. For example, current supervisors would be expected to know what their local systems and rules are, and how these are carried out in their particular faculties, schools, colleges, units or departments. Likewise, non-academic professionals and academic managers need to take seriously the argument that apparently benign systems may be harmful to the educational purposes of doctoral supervision, through shaping too severely supervisory practices.
- While aware of the potential losses changes can cause, nonetheless from this perspective, a range of activities (such as joint supervision and annual reviews) are seen as common sense, supportive measures intended to avoid getting into the kinds of relationships which this group have had most difficulty salvaging, rather than being seen as the excesses of managerialism or monitoring, even when the shortcomings of policies and systems were well recognized. Academic managers, too, reflected this macro view, but also had more detailed awareness of the complexity and potential losses of implementing a fully systemic approach to supervision.
- It has become common practice in many institutions to insist that supervisors keep notes of meetings, a practice which is irksome when it is seen purely as a bureaucratic 'back-covering' exercise. More helpful is to merge note-taking with pedagogic goals: so, for example, the tradition of asking the student to write up a meeting and circulate notes allows everyone to check out the student's understanding of what was said. Similarly, regular reviews can be a formalized version of commonsense approaches to moving research projects along. Equally as useful are 'previews' and forward planning, with wider discussions of how the student is experiencing the whole process of doctoral education.

Members of the interview group were aware that it is not enough to develop uniform processes (if, indeed, even possible) and saw clearly the limitations of policy in managing supervision; they also questioned the extent to which policies and codes of practice can dilute the innate risks for both supervisors and students in supervisory relationships. However, the relational aspect of supervision was the part that most knew, understood and experienced as weak in the worst-case scenarios. Task and vantage point in an institution are important shapers of opinion. If task had included the experience of clearing up where supervision required outside help, then opinion was likely to be against the one-to-one 'apprenticeship' form of supervision, which was seen as the most difficult to repair after the event. Hence, this group's viewpoints on supervision are substantially shaped by engagement with exceptional cases because of the primacy of 'repair' tasks. Fortunately, 'hard' cases remain in the minority. To continue the quest to understand mundane, run-of-the-mill, day-to-day supervision, we must now turn to supervisors' accounts.

Part 3
Supervisors – Old and New

Part 3 explores supervisors' perspectives. Chapter 6 draws on a national survey in which the participants indicated that they enjoyed supervision, which they saw as a responsibility as well as being central to the intellectual challenge of developing subject knowledge and understanding. They enjoyed seeing bright and enthusiastic students develop, but recognized the difficulties inherent in doctoral education.

Chapter 7 looks in detail at a group of new supervisors, asking: how do they learn to become supervisors? Once moving beyond their own doctoral experience, it is evident that new supervisors bring a range of skills and observations gathered about supervision. Most had been teaching and researching for some years before taking on their first doctoral students, as well as examining and reviewing articles for publication.

In Chapter 8, interviews with experienced supervisors recommended as 'successful' form the basis for understanding their approaches to supervision. It became evident that they held both a notion of responsiveness to each student project with a picture of the optimum journey through the PhD (I call these 'flexi-structures'). The place of criticism and criticality in supervision is discussed, along with their view of uncomfortable supervisory experience.

Supervision: A Shared View?

Chapter Outline

This chapter identifies shared themes held by supervisors, even though they are such a diverse population working in different subject areas. Supervisors expressed enjoyment of the role, saw it as a collaborative one and wider than research guidance alone; they saw student characteristics as important components in making completion possible; and new supervisors, unsurprisingly, seemed marginally less sure of their roles than experienced ones. Overall, this group enjoyed supervision, seeing it as a joint enterprise with bright, enthusiastic students and in which the intellectual challenge was to advance the subject of study through primary research and scholarship.

During this project I have been told that supervisors were too interested in their research to spend time on supervision, or that many were not interested in their students and had forgotten what it felt like to be a PGR student. Others, in the course of the study, commented on supervisors' resistance to training and to change. Further, it is standard to say that supervision is defined by discipline of study: yet, in my experience, repeating this mantra without further explanation has tended to shut down discussion rather than to open up understanding. Not least, this is because subject area and topic of study so defines the nature and isolation of each PhD that accepting this as a starting point closes off the possibility of outsiders gaining understanding of any sort. I had to believe that it was possible to find answers to the questions: what does supervision look like from the supervisors' perspective, and how do they see the issues surrounding supervising the PhD?

The story is more complex than defining supervision by subject matter alone. Supervisors are young, old, new or experienced in supervision, and they are male and female; they may be new supervisors but experienced in non-university workplaces. The PhD itself can be part time, studied at a distance or be part of a doctoral programme – all of which have implications for supervisory style as well as for the range of students. Supervisors are varied in their experience and levels of success as researchers. All these possible variations jostle for attention, before consideration of individual preferences and how these interact with specific disciplinary traditions.

To talk of 'supervisors' as if they represent a known or homogeneous population is, then, a device to enable communication on the subject of supervision, not an indication that there is a recognizable population out there waiting patiently to be researched. Rather, when it comes to engagement in supervision, there are potentially as many issues as there are supervisors, who are all shaped in turn by their personal history of supervision as well as disciplinary traditions, the format of the PhD, their avowed research paradigm, their institutional rules (on, for example, qualifications for supervision, joint supervisory teams) or the impact of particular vantage points (perhaps as supervisory team directors or deans of graduate studies).

Given that my original aim was to develop my teaching (of both PGR students and supervisors), one possible route to this information is feedback forms collected at the end of courses. My preference for feedback – especially for getting 'on-the-day' feedback from short courses – is for detailed conversations and working with course members on the exercises they do, plus detailed post-course reflection about what has happened, or has been said, as my basis for analysing courses. I have, of course, received many end-of-course feedback forms over the years. I design forms that make it hard to avoid making critical comments, rather than settling for 'happy' feedback. Forms filled in at the end of short courses, in particular, tend to reflect how comfortable one has made participants (not necessarily the most desirable learning outcome for a course); feedback asked for at a later point tends to be returned only spasmodically. Feedback forms allow people to let off steam if they want to; they allow one to dilute the unhelpful assumption that course members are on the receiving end of 'being taught', as opposed to being in a dialogue with course leaders. But they do not provide the depth of understanding I need in order to attempt to design courses that truly engage with participants' supervisory practices.

I wanted to get behind the assumed homogeneous picture of supervisors' views and allow space for myriad differences to be acknowledged, and also to see what similarities there might be. Hence, a part of this study was designed to see if it was possible to get a sense of current thinking and shared experiences among supervisors, without assuming that recent debates swirling around supervision are necessarily the major, or indeed only, possible set of attitudes or experiences. In the following two sections, I draw on two sets of data: one from 15 supervisors working in eight universities who filled in my earliest, exploratory questionnaire, and a larger national survey (to which 108 supervisors responded). The full survey included 58 attitudinal statements (using Likert scales) and seven open-ended questions.

Issues that arose in the exploratory survey were reflected in the national survey. It quickly became clear that both groups enjoy, worry about and expect to develop their supervision. They were acutely aware of the changing context in which supervision takes place, commenting on increased bureaucracy and numbers of students, coupled with workload allocation models that are optimistic when it comes to the reality of supervision. Learning to be a supervisor is seen as a developmental, experiential matter, learnt through doing rather than through having been a research student. While there was a place for some training (especially cross-disciplinary) alongside experience, established staff were generally perceived as resistant to training.

The PhD was recognized as a frustrating and lonely experience for students, whose success was seen to be made possible by students' personal characteristics (e.g. persistence and capacity to work independently) and through certain types of support, especially good supervision and fellow students. One added comment gives some insight into what this means in reality:

> The quality of the students: weak students require an incredible effort, while good students are an asset to the group and a pleasure to work with.

What follows draws on the larger survey, starting with an overview of supervisor responses. Secondly, these are then reconsidered in the light of any significant differences in responses according to three groupings: discipline, gender and supervisory experience. Finally, open-ended information is added to the descriptive statistics to explore the nature of supervision by understanding supervisors' concerns and their enjoyment of the role. Under the heading of 'family resemblances', a broad narrative of supervision can be seen as shared across all groups; yet some indication of the individual nature of each PhD and the impact of context on its individuality shows through within this shared framework.

Overview of responses: shared views

One hundred and eight supervisors from around the UK filled in my survey, drawn from over 20 universities and across arts, social science, science and management subjects. 38 per cent were female, and English was the first language of 85 per cent of respondents. Given their diversity, what commonality was there – if any – in their responses? I took 75 per cent and above (either agreement or disagreement) on any one item to represent commonality and the following picture emerged:

- 91 per cent agreed that they enjoy contact with research students
- 90 per cent agreed that supervision is time-consuming
- 94 per cent agreed that successful completion of a thesis was made possible by students' persistence
- 93 per cent agreed that completion is hampered by students' personal problems
- 92 per cent agreed that completion is hampered by poor supervision
- 90 per cent agreed that good supervision aids completion
- 90 per cent agreed that a student's resilient nature aids completion
- 86 per cent agreed that lack of funds might hamper student progress.

Whatever mismatch in communication between students and supervisors I have noted over the years, in the separate staff and student surveys both groups were in agreement as to what are the top four elements that will lead to successful completion. They were in agreement that successful completion is a mixture of student qualities and good supervision, although the supervisors were more likely to rate highly all four qualities than students did.

Table 6.1 What makes successful completion possible?

Successful completion of my thesis will be made possible because . . .	% agreed	% agreed
	Students	Staff on students' completion
(Students') persistence	96%	94%
(Students') capacity to work independently	88%	91%
(Students') resilient nature	79%	90%
Good supervision	72%	90%

Supervisors appeared to enjoy supervision, which they recognized as a wider role than just responding to students' research projects.

- 85 per cent saw involvement in students' skills' development (e.g. writing, giving presentations) as part of supervision
- 83 per cent saw the supervisory role as one that includes helping research students to publish
- 81 per cent welcomed supervising
- 81 per cent recognized the PhD as a frustrating experience
- 80 per cent saw students' career development as their concern
- 78 per cent agreed that they got to know their research students well
- 77 per cent felt confident in their supervisory style
- 76 per cent felt they should offer careers' advice as supervisors
- 75 per cent felt they had learnt from experience how to be a supervisor.

These descriptive statistics will come as little surprise to supervisors – although they may surprise their students. I looked to see if three potential areas of difference that had begun to emerge in the literature and in the exploratory questionnaires gave significantly different responses: discipline, gender and experience of supervisor.

Groups: discipline, gender and supervisor experience

The Mann-Whitney test (see Sheskin, 2004) was used to compare these three groupings to see if there were any significant differences in responses on the Likert items; and the mean responses were used to estimate the direction of shift for those items that appeared to be significant. Those significant at the 5 per cent level are reported here.

Discipline

Staff were categorized in one of four groups: science and technology, arts and social science, management, and medicine (including health and nursing). Ten items showed as significant when examined for discipline differences in response.

- All agreed that supervision is challenging – but management were most likely to agree, and science and technology were slightly less likely to agree.

- All agreed that supervision is time-consuming – management were most likely to agree, followed by arts and social science, whereas science and technology were least likely to agree.
- All tended to agree that work commitments hamper students' progress, but management were most likely to agree, and medicine least likely to agree.
- All agree that supervisors should provide careers advice although medicine were least likely to agree and management were most likely to agree.
- All agreed (but tended towards neutral) that a supportive family helped student completion – management were most likely to agree, and arts and social science least likely to agree.
- All tended to agree that supervisors should work collaboratively with students – but science and technology were most likely to agree, while arts and social science were least likely to agree.
- All tended to agree that it was part of their role to help students publish – but science and technology were most likely to agree, and medicine least likely to agree.
- All agree that supervisors should publish jointly with students – science and technology were most likely to agree, and arts and social science were least likely to agree.
- All tended to agree that they had learnt about supervision from students they have supervised – but science and technology were most likely to agree, and medicine least likely to agree.
- Science and technology were most likely to agree that they expect to see students once a fortnight – while medicine tended towards disagreement, followed by arts and social science who tended towards neutral on this item.

Gender

Seven of the Likert items showed significant differences in response by gender:

- All tended to agree that they are confident in their supervision style – but men were more likely to agree than women.
- All tended to agree that they have learnt from experience how to be a supervisor – but men were more likely to agree than women.
- All agreed that they are likely to learn about supervision from students they have supervised – but men are more likely to agree than women.
- All agreed that their role includes helping research students to get published – but men were more likely than women to agree.
- All agreed that supervisors should co-publish with students, but men were more likely to agree than women.
- Men were more likely to agree that they see students once a fortnight, whereas women were closer to neutral (neither agree nor disagree).

Supervisor experience

Nine items showed as significant when examined for differences between experienced and new supervisors (defined by respondents' choice of category):

- Experienced supervisors tended towards disagreement with the item 'I learnt most about supervision from being a student'; whereas new supervisors tended towards agreement (although were close to neutral).
- Both agreed that they learnt from experience about supervision – but experienced supervisors were much more likely to agree with this.
- Experienced supervisors were much more likely than inexperienced supervisors to agree that they have learnt to supervise from students they have supervised.
- Experienced supervisors are much less likely than inexperienced ones to have attended supervisor training.
- Experienced supervisors were more likely to agree that they expect to see students once a fortnight than inexperienced ones, although both groups tended towards agreement with this item.
- Both sets agreed, but experienced supervisors were much more likely than inexperienced ones to feel 'under examination when my students reach their viva'.
- While both tended to agree that supportive families help completion, experienced supervisors were less likely to agree.
- While both agreed that good supervision aids student completion, experienced supervisors were slightly less likely to agree with this.
- Both groups agreed that funding helps completion, but experienced supervisors were less inclined to agree that it did.

What is of interest, of course, is how few items show significant difference in responses and how easily those that do might be understood as the result of a number of other, interacting elements beyond discipline, gender or experience alone, such as: stage in career, age, access to supervisory experience, and subject-related styles of supervision and research, involvement in doctoral programmes and access to team research. Indeed, a simple cross-tabulation of the variables gender, discipline and supervisor experience show that in this group of respondents science and technology supervisors were most likely to be experienced supervisors and to be male, and hence understanding of many differences in responses follow from this. In this study, women are more likely to be new supervisors and to be in arts and social science subjects. So the results indicate that those with more experience learn from experience and from students who they have seen through to vivas. Collaboration and publication with students, however, appears more likely to be indicative of broad cultural difference between subject areas.

Supervisor–student relationship: concerns and enjoyment

I have noticed students falter many times, over the years, as I ask what they hope for from their supervisors. They want something more than distant, academic tutoring but, they tell me, they are not looking for friendship. Yet they do hope for interest and some level of closeness, what might be described as 'intellectual friendship', in which the joys and disappointments of research are shared. It is, in that sense, an intense and close relationship. In open-ended questions, supervisors volunteered their picture of supervision by describing concerns and what makes supervision an enjoyable part of academic work.

Concerns

Supervisors, too, expect closeness or, at least, recognize the potential intensity in supervision: they expect to take high levels of responsibility, take time, share knowledge, provide opportunities and act as gatekeepers in students' futures. 94 per cent agreed that supervision is challenging. 71 per cent agreed that they had, in the past, worried about supervision while 46 per cent currently worry. 61 per cent agreed that they felt under examination when their students reach vivas. 66.6 per cent viewed research students as 'apprentice academics'. 56 per cent agreed that they should work collaboratively with students (63 per cent agreed that students should be able to manage their own work). How did supervisors summarize their concerns about supervision? Time, responsibility, knowledge and choice of students were all concerns that were volunteered in the open-ended questions – or some mixture of these key areas, and in this they reflected McMichael's work (1993) in spite of the passage of time and changes that have occurred in the last decade.

Time

Time was a concern to this group: 90 per cent had agreed that supervision is time-consuming. 50 per cent agreed that they see students at least once a fortnight (25 per cent disagreed). Of course, with part-time and doctoral programme students, such a regime would be unrealistic, plus:

> In my experience, you see students at irregular intervals, and should. You need to see them more in Year 1. They think they need to see you more during the writing-up stage or prior to upgrading. They are usually right in this.

Institutional guidelines and student expectations about frequency of meetings may reflect other agendas. How such decisions are made rest on a variety of considerations, not least the nature of the student's project. Time, however, was rarely the sole concern:

> I did not tick the 'at least once a fortnight' question because of the necessity in my discipline to be away at archives. I would have ticked 'regularly' and 'several times a term in most circumstances', however. My other concerns are usually about my ability to supervise the specific research topic: I am happiest when supervising closer to my own expertise, but this has not always been the case in my job when I have co-supervised research that was only peripherally related to my knowledge.

Others, too, expressed discomfort at supervising away from their core subject area (see 'knowledge' below), raising questions about how comfortable they felt with joint supervision in which, on occasions, it is possible to be only tangentially aligned with the research project.

A desire to do the job well led one to express concern that there is a:

> . . . perception that PhD supervision is somehow a perk of the job and not the most demanding and exacting form of the job itself. So I expect to be allocated sufficient time to supervise in a way that is truly engaged and not perfunctory.

59 per cent of respondents in this survey agreed, however, that 'supervision is one of the rewards of the job'. But they may well agree with the following summary:

> I feel that it isn't really given enough recognition on workloads – I put a lot of effort into my research students. I probably give a bit too much sometimes, so a concern I have is that I am too directive and sometimes make students dependent on me. Recently I have learned to sit back a little more and give them space to do the thinking . . . my concerns are probably about getting it right for each individual student, because they're all different.

And another commented on the competing demands of academe:

> The all-round demands these days of being an academic who also cares about what he/she does, means that there is not enough time to do any of the jobs one does with the degree of attention they deserve. I feel this most strongly in areas which relate to other human beings, whether students or colleagues, and because one probably spends more regular time with research students than any others, one feels the sorts of worries I have most keenly in relation to them, no matter how much help and support you give.

More commented on how there was only limited time to read or time to spend on research students (especially when coupled with supervising areas in which they have limited knowledge), having to pressure students to meet deadlines and a general sense of not being able to control what time they have at their disposal and spend on research students. One said:

> Isolation – both for me and the student. The growing burden of paperwork and the failure of institutions to recognize sufficiently the work involved in successful supervision (anyone can supervise badly on the basis of 10 hours per year!).

Clearly, then, some were struggling with a 'university' picture of how supervision should be carried out and the time allowed for it.

Responsibility

These supervisors had a strong sense of responsibility towards their students, and their concerns included 'letting the student down', being 'devastated' if a student failed, 'never knowing how much intervention is appropriate', offering the wrong advice, trying to be helpful in the right sort of ways, and a profound recognition that getting it wrong could 'screw up' students' lives. Two summarized this last fear:

> Having someone's whole future, in a sense, in one's hands – failures in PhD supervision can irreparably damage a student's prospects.
> My putting in great effort and students not being able to progress for various reasons. Then their dropping out, so both my and their time wasted.

One described a sense of isolation in sitting with this responsibility, and their limited feelings of control with regard to student progression:

> Lack of support when things go wrong, if a student fails to keep in touch or complete tasks and then fails to make progress, you feel you will be blamed even though you have tried to keep them on the right path.

Responsibility for students' futures via success in the PhD is made all the more important by the extended time-frame of the doctoral degree, which in turn heightens the concern to ensure students receive the right advice:

> That the guidance offered is appropriate, given the long lead-in to examination. The alignment between the necessary methodology and the student's capacity to manage this.

Always, then, supervisors return to the importance of partnership with students, and their dependency on students' ability to manage the intellectual challenge. Many supervisors had added comments about 'student ability' and 'intellectual ability' as key to successful supervision. Hence, students who are not really capable of doing a PhD rated high on the list of concerns:

> The possibility of taking on a student who is not quite capable of doing the research and writing needed for a successful thesis.
>   The pressure to take on students who you suspect aren't committed enough to deliver a thesis on time.

Attitude and independence were rated as important characteristics in capable students as were illustrated by these concerns:

> Students wanting to be told what to do every step of the way and not taking responsibility for their research – dependency.
>   Students who are not ready to work independently. Occasional disagreements with other member of supervision team.

In contrast, '*pleasant*' supervision was made possible by students who are '*receptive and critical*', rather than being '*dependent or antagonistic*'.

Knowing enough

One respondent summarized what fear of not knowing enough means to supervisors:

> Given that PhD students are operating at the frontiers of knowledge, I worry about the adequacy of my familiarity with the student's subject field.

For in many subjects, a successful student works in new areas and becomes the expert in that area, ending their doctoral education by outstripping their supervisor's knowledge. Hence, another commented on their concern that they might not have '*sufficient subject specific knowledge*'; where another feared being '*asked to supervise work with a methodology outside my area of expertise*'. Discomfort at the results of other people's recruitment practices highlighted the limited sense of control or agency felt by some:

> Pressure to supervise students who fall well outside of my own research interests. The amount of time it takes to comment on drafts written by students with poor English and/or writing skills – copy editing should not be the responsibility of a research supervisor.

Lack of knowledge (or experience) about being able to make effective judgements as a supervisor was expressed as a concern, especially if the topic for research is outside their comfort zone:

> Being able to adapt the correct approach to my student. Some students need pressure, others encouragement. Not everyone will do their PhD in the same way I did. I sometimes worry that I'm not an expert in the field they're looking at.

Responsiveness to students' needs was recognized not just as interpersonal skills, but as an outcome of experience and subject knowledge. One expressed concern that they did not have '*sufficient experience to understand when a student is making progress, and when to give someone their head*', and another described their wish to be '*effective and supportive while remaining critical and constructive*'.

Enjoyment

Supervisors were asked to volunteer what they found enjoyable in research. Echoing Vilkinas's (2008) Australian sample, they enjoyed sharing the intellectual journey with bright students, watching them develop and do well, while extending their own understanding of a subject area. One succinctly summarized the common view (expressed with some variation by nearly 70 per cent of survey respondents):

1. Learning properly about topics which I thought I knew about.
2. Seeing research students develop the confidence to become their own people and to engage in debate with both peers and seniors.
3. Seeing students I have supervised thrive either in academic life or in a career in which they make use of their research and enquiry skills.

They valued contact with bright, intelligent students solving research and methodological problems and watching them grow in confidence. One described it as an:

> Opportunity to see a young academic develop in various ways, including in their research and writing, but also their confidence. Helping a student to really get into their research and learning from them as they gradually become the expert on the subject.

And another, similarly, said:

> Watching the work grow and the ideas form, seeing an individual extend themselves and grow, engaging in proper detailed academic discussion, the sense of achievement when they complete and /or get the job they wanted.

Enjoyment came from student's enthusiasm and success, but also in engagement with varied routes to developing their joint subject area:

> The level of engagement with each individual student's personal path to success. Very varied 'biographies'. I think the teaching which a supervisor does is the nearest approximation there is to a genuine educational process in contemporary HE.
>
> With a good student working on an interesting topic, the sense of shared discovery and the intellectual excitement of new thinking.
>
> Sharing in being at the cutting-edge of research; seeing a student develop into an independent researcher over the course of their studies. From the little experience I have had of this, I am also immensely proud of my former students as they develop their (academic) careers and any role I may have played in enabling that.

Excitement was expressed concerning students' success, especially those that later became colleagues.

> Probably my best conversations about research from week to week are with research students, rather than colleagues, because there isn't really enough time to talk about research more generally, and often my interests are closer to research students' interests than those of my colleagues. It's great when someone has success – giving a paper, getting published, getting the PhD of course, building a career and ultimately becoming a colleague.

21 per cent had agreed that supervisors should become friends with students, but 53 per cent neither agreed nor disagreed – reflecting the ambivalence around this issue that was noted with students in Chapter 4. It is common

advice to tell new supervisors that they should not be 'friends' with students, because this makes it hard to give negative feedback. But Boucher and Smyth (2004) illustrate how obvious rules are not always relevant across the board and in all situations. There is no homogeneous population of postgraduates these days: as well as new graduates, PGR students may be doing doctoral programmes while they continue working; they may be doing doctorates in the workplace; they may be part of an ongoing research project; and they might be colleagues from outside the UK. As such, while many full-time PGR students do not, in the end, become academics, there are many others who are colleagues during their time of registration, either in the same or from other institutions or from part of a wider practitioner world. As colleagues, the supervisor and student are likely to remain a part of each others' worlds for some time to come.

Boucher and Smyth make clear that their supervisory work is based on closeness and that in their model, supervision is a psychological, emotional space in which to analyse practice in depth and to bring about change:

> . . . occurs within the context of relationship, not disconnected from it. It is about engagement, interaction and connection in ways that go beyond the intellectual and the surface. (p. 346)

Because of the nature of practice-based work, they illustrate how boundary issues can arise in numerous ways when supervising mature practitioners in highly reflective ways. Many of their students have already established a close relationship with them through educational, consultancy or research work (presumably a part of why they choose PGR work as an option for them), some considered as friends. To manage the potential boundary and power problems means that the supervisory relationship as well as the content of study requires negotiation (p. 348). Working through the supervisor–student relationship in this framework models the sorts of analysis that might well happen in the work-based research. It does, however, require high-level nego-tiating skills on the part of both students and staff.

Boucher and Smyth discuss a model of supervision based on supervisors accepting the humanity of students within the process of intellectual develop-ment, yet choices are shaped not just by personal preference and by subject matter but also by academic context. This group of respondents expressed a preference for responsiveness to students and flexibility in decisions (e.g. about frequency of meetings, approaches to styles of working). They also made it plain that while they prefer independent, bright, literate and receptive students who can be critical and motivated, reality meant they experienced only limited agency in controlling the context for supervision. So, for example while some subjects attract few doctoral students (further accreditation and development may be within a professional arena instead), and hence students may well be current and future colleagues, in other subjects supervisors are running large, international doctoral programmes. In such situations, numbers of students will be divided up and allocated to staff, allowing little time for close relationships to develop and limited opportunities for staff to select students. Whatever the personal and professional preferences of the staff and students concerned, the relationship may be more like that of supervisor of Master's dissertations.

Supervisory teaching goals and practices are not necessarily transparent and shared – why a supervisor behaves in certain ways may not make sense to the student, and vice versa. Woodhouse (2002), for example, describes how, at Master's level, the supervisor's intention to facilitate students in coming up with their own answers can be at odds with students' wishes to be instructed, especially in the early stages of a project (p.139). Fundamental assumptions about interactions – in this case, ways of asking and answering questions – are based on both staff and students' prior assumptions about what the interchange is intended to achieve. Pole and Sprokkereef (1997) argue that the impact of context on supervision is not only systemic, but dependent on stage of progress in the PhD. Their study illustrates the confusion and uncertainty new doctoral students experienced about the role of supervisors, making a clear expression of the expectations hard to achieve. This was the case even with those who had, as undergraduates, been high achievers within the departments in which they studied as PhD students, hence might reasonably have been said to be familiar with those circumstances (p. 52). Hence, both student and supervisor can be said to socialize each other into their roles over the time of the PhD.

Implications for supervision

- There was a shared narrative about supervision among supervisors. They generally expressed enjoyment of supervision and expected to get to know their students well in collaborative relationships in which they learn from good students and expect a wider guidance role (including skills' development and careers). Change, however, was on people's minds, leading to comments about increased

Implications for supervision—Cont'd

bureaucracy and formalization of the supervision process. Comments, too, were made about motivating weak students and concerns were expressed about pressure to take on less able students. Enjoyment of the role arises out of its centrality to academic endeavour: solving research problems at the edge of disciplinary knowledge with bright, enthusiastic students. There is, then, a framework within which information, strategies and experiences of supervision can be shared across groups.

- The risks for supervisors lay in their dependency on students to fulfil their part in taking the project forward. Key academic dispositions reappeared: independence, criticality and robust motivation were problematic when missing from students, especially in the later stages of doctoral education. While this group were acutely aware of their responsibilities, university pressures (external to the supervisor and experienced as beyond their control) were also referred to in responses: holding supervisors to account for unsuccessful students and recruiting greater numbers of PGR students, and providing the context in which supervisors moved outside their comfort area vis-a-vis students' subject matter. How supported new supervisors, in particular, feel in this environment is an important question for the development of future academics with the confidence and experience to work creatively at the edge of their disciplines.

- While there is a shared narrative about supervision, this does not mean that the detailed, contextualized narrative of each supervisory story is not relevant. Quite the opposite, for subject matter remains the essential education, indeed it *is* the PhD. A shared narrative within which academic dispositions are defined provides a framework for understanding and analysing the supervision of the doctorate as an educational experience, whose challenges are entirely contextualized within subject matter. While information is limited in this analysis about the groups explored (gender, discipline and supervisor experience) nonetheless they indicate ways in which practising supervisors can ask themselves further questions to reflect on their experience of the interaction of these factors with their area of study.

- Different skills are required of supervisors at different points in the process and high-level relational and communication skills are needed on the part of both supervisors and students engaged in this teaching relationship. Among the key themes, change is felt to have been at work and yet supervision has remained a form of developmental tutorship that was – at its best – expected to be collaborative and to go beyond research guidance alone. Most importantly, supervision is a form of developmental tutoring that is mediated through subject matter, located in the power relations of specific, international fields of study while administered within local, academic departments. Yet, as we saw, conscientious supervisors were struggling to juggle the tensions and to retain this picture of supervision within the time constraints and workload allocation models being used.

My original questions were defined as educational ones: how do both supervisors and students develop and learn their crafts? It has become clear that there are shared narratives between supervisors about the place, nature and enjoyment of supervision in their working lives; and there are shared concerns about time and responsibility in a changing environment (not least, one in which many seemed to feel little control over the elements for which they are held to account). There are shared expectations between supervisors about the academic dispositions they anticipate will be apparent in successful PhD students. What is less clear is how young academics move from being a recent doctoral graduate to becoming a supervisor and what skills they learn, or where they learn them from. The easy assumption that all supervisors reflect their own experience (either in copying it or in reacting against it) is beginning to appear too simplistic in the light of this data. So, in the next chapter, I turn to interviews with new supervisors to explore these questions in more detail.

7 Learning to be a Supervisor

How do people learn to supervise and what do 'novice' supervisors bring to supervision? As this chapter illustrates, being a novice supervisor does not mean coming to supervision without relevant experience. New supervisors have developed a range of relevant skills over time and draw on their personal experience as PhD students, time in academe watching colleagues, acting as reviewers and as members of panels examining student progress. In this chapter, their experience, doubts and expectations are explored, along with their intentions for supervisory styles.

For students there can be advantages to working with staff who are new to supervision. New supervisors can bring freshness and enthusiasm, openness to the experience, up-to-date knowledge and may have undergone some level of training. New supervisors may also enjoy universities as they are currently constituted, and be less concerned with how much life has changed and what life was like in the past. Plus, throughout this project, respondents made it clear that novice supervisors are perceived to be more egalitarian and able to work alongside students, and that students who can benefit from such an energetic, sharing approach gain opportunities to develop intellectual independence.

Conversely, we have already heard that new supervisors may be slower to define when students are facing real difficulties (see Chapter 1) and necessarily call on a narrower experience base when making these judgements. However, as we have seen in Chapter 4, a 'threshold concepts' approach illustrates the complex nature of learning making it hard to distinguish between the inherent difficulties attached to key developmental challenges and what (perhaps retrospectively) is defined as insurmountable difficulty. Novice supervisors are less likely to have read many theses in the subject area, and are negotiating their way through the power relations of their departments and research communities from an unequal position. Alignment of institutional requirements with departmental ones is mediated by issues of power – such as, for example, the new supervisors' positioning within national and international research communities and in relation to powerful individuals within their sections.

However, of late there is more support for new supervisors: in most universities it is no longer enough just to be employed as an academic. New supervisors are expected to attend training courses, and are highly likely to be members of supervisory teams led by a director who has already experienced success in seeing research students through to vivas. This provides protection for both supervisors and students by recognizing the gradual acquisition of supervisory skills that are needed beyond subject knowledge alone. For the supervisors, however, it means that the process of 'becoming' works at three levels:

- Through opportunities to develop experience by finding students to assist or co-supervise.
- Adjusting to local teaching requirements and practices within an institution and within their own section or department's practices.
- While positioning themselves within their external reference groups (national and international research and disciplinary communities) and their standards, from which external examiners will be drawn and within which they too will become examiners.

Of course, these three levels are not watertight compartments, but interact and shape each other. Hakala (2009) analyses the socialization of researchers in Finland within the context of changing political and funding demands, allowing for 'junior' (PhD students) and senior researchers. Borrowing Hakala's implicit continuum of stages in becoming a researcher, it is clear that novices start supervision at all points along the way. Novice supervisors gather a portfolio of relevant experience: supervising undergraduate and Master's dissertations, supporting doctoral students for part of their studies (e.g. supporting writing up), taking on supervision for limited periods (during a colleagues' illness, sabbatical or travels), or joining established supervisory teams when other supervisors become unavailable, perhaps because they have moved universities. Other experience adds to the portfolio of supervisory skills, such as taking part in student review panels (these are named differently according to institutions), reviewing for peer-reviewed journals or being an internal examiner.

Levels of support may depend on local circumstances, as Amundsen and McAlpine (2009) observed is the case in two universities in Canada: 'While both institutions had policies regarding when new academics could begin supervising doctoral students, these were not referred to and did not appear to be followed' (p. 333). It is difficult to write meaningful policies that apply to all eventualities (see Grant), and guidelines are preferable: departments may not have the spare capacity to follow policies to the letter, and implementation may require choices to accommodate the shifts and changes in university staffing. Further, how students are recruited is relevant to how novice supervisors gather their first students. Some prospective students apply to a department and are allocated according to individual supervisor interests, while others apply direct to individual staff for entry to a department. In many science subjects, students are recruited to carry out specific aspects of externally funded projects, so acceptance means joining a team.

Behind these differences are distinct cultures about supervisors and their position vis-à-vis subject knowledge. Where *institutions* favour joint supervision or supervisory teams (in line with the QAA guidelines), *disciplinary cultures* can still be rooted in the tradition that sees supervisors as individual subject masters. Yet, in spite of its longevity, such an individualized culture of supervision is not always sustainable: subject areas change and develop over a lifetime and so supervisors, too, broaden their interests – occasionally out of personal development but perhaps, also, out of pragmatism in focusing on areas that are relevant to more students. Similarly, supervisory teams require a broader set of expectations about supervisory roles and tasks, rather than expecting a team to be made up solely of subject experts.

Whatever support systems are in place, new supervisors may still be gathering experience with students in recognizably complex situations. It is not easy to take over supervision from someone else. Coming in as a 'new' person (new to the team, new to academe, recognized as less expert and less experienced) where relationships have been established puts novice supervisors at a disadvantage. Holligan (2005) has described the frustration of supervising where agreements have already been made about research design, ways of working and managing meetings. He lacked knowledge '. . . of the student's preferred learning styles and pre-existing levels of expertise', and was unaware of the student's construction of 'the wider environment of academe within which the "drama" of supervision plays out' (p. 270). Where the student works at a distance (a common occurrence these days), there are few informal opportunities to unravel misunderstandings or grievances. If the student has already experienced changes of supervision or is having problems with their PhD, new supervisors can find themselves managing tricky situations that require high-level personal and intellectual skills.

Holligan became aware of a need to deconstruct his prior research experience and to question both its relevance to his new student and how his research knowledge could be usefully communicated (p. 270). In what follows, I am asking similar questions by exploring the ways in which these novice supervisors developed relevant expertise; what sorts of student experience they bring to supervision; how new supervisors learn from colleagues; and, finally, consider their expectations of supervision as a way of contextualizing supervisor development.

Developing expertise: being a new supervisor

It is not entirely clear what constitutes newness in supervision. Hence, it is not obvious how supervisors learn their craft, nor how to design courses that prepare supervisors for these challenging beginnings. Supervising PhDs comes to people at all points in their careers, and being a novice supervisor is a stage that is not necessarily the same as being inexperienced either in academe or in other work places. As a simple definition, 'novice' supervisors in this project had not supervised or co-supervised one student through to successful completion of a viva within the UK. But this in no way constitutes 'beginners' in the sense of arriving at supervision without relevant experience. Novice supervisors arrive at my courses agreeing with the mantra that they should attend, but with hugely different skills' sets and expectations.

Ten men and 11 women filled in background, 'novice' questionnaires, and their answers illustrated this variety of experience and needs in novice supervisors. They were aged between 26 and 50, with the majority in their 30s and 40s, although most had been students within the preceding ten years. Between them, they had done their previous degrees at a total of at least 12 universities around the UK, plus two outside the UK. Reflecting the increasingly international character of UK universities, English was the first language for 14, while the remaining seven spoke German, Arabic, Greek, Russian or Danish as their first languages. So, while accepting the definition of 'new supervisors', they nonetheless represented a range of university and international experience. Six interviewees inform this chapter: three women and three men were drawn from science and technology subjects (three) and arts or social science subjects (three). For two, English was not their first language – one coming from the Middle East, while the other came from Scandinavia.

The following four fictional profiles illustrate the range of experience that novice supervisors bring to supervision tasks. They are drawn from a mixture of the research material described here, plus extensive conversations with supervisors on courses and at conferences across the UK. These vignettes indicate the challenge for designers of courses for supervisors, given the variety of skills' sets and first supervisory tasks, even though colleagues are in agreement that new supervisors require training. They show the importance for new supervisors of reflecting on their work context, their skills' sets and their need to work out (individually) the best ways to develop further.

1. For Anya, supervision was still an abstract task that she had not yet done, but was thinking about because after 12 years of scientific postdoctoral work, she was putting in her own applications for grants. Her experience of research had ranged from her PhD, when she was 'just plonked down in the lab' without the necessary skills or support to learn them, through to working in highly motivated, successful teams. Postdoc supervision had been in dynamic teams where multiple grants were run by a research-entrepreneur, who nonetheless found time to be more accessible than her PhD supervisor. In this environment her skills developed, successfully publishing and producing conference papers and, importantly, she became senior researcher with responsibility for day-to-day supervision of research. Hence, she saw post-doc supervision as knowing how much of the research is going to plan, to be accessible to discuss work and ideas, to hold regular meetings, be ready to pick up the 'sideshoots' that will turn into future grant applications. The PhD, she said, is the 'youth training scheme' of science, whether graduates stay in academe or not. The PhD supervisor in this model provides the framework, the research focus (and the money) and runs parallel strands simultaneously, while the post-doc supervisor is engaged in the daily detail of projects.

So what makes her a novice supervisor, other than the technicality of not being a named supervisor for graduate PhD students? Anya illustrates how postdoctoral work in teams adds another layer of experience and model of supervision on which to draw. So, she is already publishing, writing grants, running projects and highly developed in her research specialism. In her eyes, the key skills less exercised are interpersonal and management, which she sees as highly dependent on personality: '. . . one can attend as many courses on supervising people as you want, but if you haven't got the personality, if you are not a nice person and are not approachable then I really don't think that is going to change it.' In addition to supervisor's personality, she felt success depended very much on what the student was like and what they brought to research.

2. Ben is an applied science specialist and had taken on joint supervision of a student some eighteen months into the project when the first supervisor had moved universities. The supervision is joint across two departments, although in practice the co-supervisor saw Ben's research expertise as the most relevant so did not engage unduly; however, there were differences in the two departments' expectations of students at different stages in the PhD and this was reflected in how they used their review systems. The student was also a part-time student who worked away from the university. Ben felt email supervision was not working, so instigated Skype conversations (allowing more informal development of discussion) as well as meeting if Ben was travelling near to the student's home or work.

Ben had been researching into the student's area for some ten years, and had only recently transferred from research posts to a permanent lectureship. Prior to that he had been self-directing in managing the projects on which he worked, published successfully and was known for recent innovations in the area via a conference network. He felt unable to redirect the decisions already made about the shape of the student's project, but brought up-to-date literature and knowledge to the work.

Most difficulties were slowly being overcome with goodwill on both sides. The rest, he felt, would be managed when he could recruit students himself, and so influence the planning of a project from the beginning. He had concerns about what university rules and regulations around supervision might be, but felt that his basic level teaching course had helped him to reflect constructively on teaching in ways that would support his supervisory work.

3. Cas was a mathematician with one student, recruited by her and part-way through the first year of their PhD. Cas has worked at a number of universities in the UK, teaching and researching as well as completing her own PhD. Unlike

experimental sciences, with which she compared her work, maths' researchers cannot say in advance what methods will be used to solve certain problems – indeed, knowing the methods only arises when solutions have been found.

As a supervisor, it is her job to find the right problems to point students to and to provide the scaffolding that will enable students to work towards solutions. To provide, too, knowledge of who is working on similar problems and entrée to networks that offset the inherent isolation and independent tradition of mathematics research. This tradition is at odds with notions of joint supervision and set timeframes (it can take a long time to see if work comes to fruition and there are few guarantees of success). As there can be no university training programme for supervisors in the maths problems under study, it is hard for Cas to see what might be helpful other than ticking the box that one has attended. Cas herself drew confidence for supervising from the mentoring system her section had set up between established and novice supervisors.

4. Dieter had five years' worth of postdoctoral research in an arts subject, and had just started to supervise a student who had already started, but whose supervisor had moved universities. The student was part time and lived away from the university, and the subject is one that Dieter had once been interested in but his own research agenda had moved on from. The supervision was 50-50 with a senior colleague, and he had worries about how much time his professorial colleague could really commit to the student. The supervision was conducted substantially by email with occasional Skype conversations, with all the key decisions about the project having being taken with people who had long gone.

Dieter was an independent researcher, much travelled and published. His own PhD supervisor had left part-way through his studies, and personal determination had seen him through. While, from his own experience, he knew that doing a PhD without a research culture can be hard, he also accepted isolation as part of the nature of research:

> I think that's just the way it is, it's the same when you have a job and in departments you have people specializing in different areas, so it's just another area of academic specialization.

Being happy in your life was something that supported research in his view, and having access to national and international networks to support the work.

Training, for Dieter, was useful if it addressed power relations in research supervision, *'because unfortunately some academics are like that'*.

Many novice supervisors, then, have sophisticated skills' sets relevant to the tasks of supervision and none are starting at precisely the same level of knowledge; and any individual development plan would need to be highly personalized to be effective. Yet in Chapter 6 it became apparent that there were some, albeit limited, differences between experienced and new supervisors in their responses to the national survey. There were few surprises: not least, new supervisors drew on their experience of being supervised, where experienced supervisors were able to draw on a history of working with a range of students. This echoed a set of related beliefs about novice supervisors that was repeated to me regularly: that people supervise as they were supervised and that those who go onto academe as careers have had good experiences as doctoral students. Amundsen and McAlpine (2009) situate the experience of novice supervisors 'within the broader context of undertaking to establish oneself as an academic' (p. 332); and within this interview group, that process had clearly started while they were completing their PhDs.

Drawing on past experience: being a doctoral student

Certainly, the novice questionnaire group had, on the whole, experienced good supervision, as became apparent when asked what they would like to do that is the same as their supervisor: *'Have the same high expectations'*; *'Like my supervisor, I want to give my students freedom to develop their own ideas independently'*; *'Be inspirational'*; *'Be approachable'*; *'Show respect for my student. Provide positive but critical feedback'*; *'Provide ideas and enthusiasm'*; and *'Be flexible and responsive to student needs as my supervisor was. Offer some structure in the planning of research. Offer some support in career choices.'*

While clear about what their supervisors had done well, there was also clarity about what had not worked for them and, hence, what they would hope to do differently. For, rather than experiencing only good supervision, they echoed the recent graduates (see Chapter 3) in that the good never offset bad: *'My supervisor was always warm, caring, gentle and supportive. I would hope to be, mostly, if not always, the same. However, I felt my supervisor was not critical enough of my work, thus left me feeling unprepared to deal with criticism – I would hope to provide more critical commentary on written text/ideas/progress/*

research practice.' Others would have valued a more 'hands-on' approach, which one summarized as:

> Be supportive, approachable. Devote more time to my students and especially provide better feedback following discussions and written work. Provide better guidance on useful, up-to-date literature and information sources.

On a similar theme of greater involvement, others commented: *'More regular meetings – be more pro-active in recommending readings and help structure writing'*; *'Meet more regularly'*; *'Not to be absent for first three months – not to get tied up in personal life and neglect student'*; *'Get involved more often in helping the student overcome obstacles, intellectual or otherwise'*; *'Focus students on the importance of getting good publishable data'*; *'Better-inform student about available training opportunities'*; *'Greater support on a day-to-day basis'*; *'More interest, encouragement, but good understanding of when to chase/leave me alone.'*

The interview group showed how novice supervisors can still remember exactly how complicated being supervised can feel on occasions. Five of the six interviewees described difficulties in their experiences as doctoral students: supervisors changed, left, one became seriously ill and others just proved problematic. Whatever the difficulties, they described how they had used all the resources at their disposal (including their growing understanding of how the academic world operates) to ensure their success.

One was clear that supervisors should maintain a commitment to their students even when they move posts, presenting an image of supervisor as responsible beyond the confines of a specific job or institution. This had been the behaviour of her original supervisor who had moved to the United States for a new job. This conceptualization of supervision is related to the primary membership of researchers to an international research community rather than to a local institution. While, in this case, their relationship had not been ideal, with too few meetings held at irregular intervals, *'so it was unregulated, too distant'*, the supervisor had continued to read material even after leaving. As a research student, this novice supervisor had turned to friends and acquaintances in the field to manage the rest of her PhD:

> We had a mutual friend who taught me when I was an undergraduate and I knew my [second] supervisor, she was at another university, but she kindly agreed to take on the bulk of supervision and also was very instrumental in finding me an external examiner.

Such friendships call into question the mixed thinking around whether or not supervisors and their students should form friendships (see chapters 4 and 6). It may be a function of age and stage in career, but 'friendship' might also be a marker of a student already partially socialized into an academic career, defined as a promising colleague rather than a problem student.

Another novice supervisor's PhD had also been made possible by a friend's supervision, after a rocky beginning. He described the start of his doctoral experience:

> I was accepted on the scholarship, and the minute I arrived it was really clear that I should never have been accepted because there was nobody to supervise me. I was given one supervisor for the first year and then he left and so then I got another one and he just said 'I just don't know anything about what you're doing', and I didn't know anything about what I was doing, so I just basically spent 18 months reading things in the library, just not having a clue.

After 18 months he left for work at another, and then another, university. For four years he went on collecting material for a PhD but was not registered anywhere or supervised. He watched what his partner was asked to do by supervisors, and tried to incorporate that into his work. In the end, the process of 'becoming an academic' made completion of the PhD possible:

> By that point I was really good friends with the person who then became my supervisor . . . At the same time as I was doing my PhD I was learning to be an academic as well, so I was writing on different areas and getting those published; I knew I could write and I think what she did was give me the real confidence that I could pull it all together and that was the biggest thing she did for me.

Having a work colleague as supervisor brings its own issues (as was illustrated in chapters 3 and 4). Denicolo (2004) discusses supervision of colleagues within the same department and institution, which means that student and supervisor meet each other in their multiple roles within academe (teachers, knowledge expert, administrators and managers). So, the closeness of working lives for colleague supervisor-students means the relationship is positioned within a set of hierarchies and power relations, additional to the usual supervisor–student ones. For example, focusing on the intellectual and overlooking the emotional was seen as potentially problematic, as some colleague-students felt 'vulnerable sharing their private worries with a fellow colleague, especially if either of them was in a more senior position for other academic activities or was of a different gender' (p. 703). In contrast with Hunt (see Chapter 4), emotional openness enabled completion of this novice supervisor's PhD, not least because the supervisor-friend understood the student's sensitivities so well: their existing collegial friendship had been established, allowing the supervisor to accept the student's emotionality about the PhD to be absorbed into supervision rather than to continue to be a barrier to progress.

A third had been so unhappy with her supervision that she had, at the time, complained. This, in her experience, had made matters worse (*'she wasn't a particularly nice character, and she wasn't at all approachable'*) and requests for a new supervisor were refused

> My supervisor there was very seldom around . . . I had very little theoretical teaching and even less hands-on practical teaching. At undergraduate level your practical experience is limited, so what you really do need when you start a PhD is a few weeks, few months maybe, hands-on experience by the supervisor in the laboratory.

She made the comparison with later, good supervision as a postdoctoral student:

> [my postdoctoral supervisor] was far busier than my [doctoral] supervisor. He was already much more senior, a lot more administrative work, he also had a large research group when I joined, better established. We had monthly meetings . . . to check the progress and for him to pick on ideas, and in addition to the formal meetings you would chat with him in the corridor and knock on his office door and he was always there. It was far more constructive for both parties, also a much nicer chap as well, character-wise.

In contrast, she now saw her first supervisor as working below-par and unlikely to succeed in the current climate, but such a judgement had not been possible for her to make when choosing to study for her doctorate.

Similarly, a fourth novice supervisor had learnt a model of supervision from his postdoctoral experience not open to him when studying for his doctorate. Then he had not got on with his supervisor, but (unlike above), had not doubted his supervisor's competence; in addition, he made use of a lively and active research environment to offset difficulties with his supervisor:

> I don't think we got on terribly well, or it was a bit of a mismatch, and I never felt I got terribly much support from him but I was lucky to be in a very friendly department . . . where other people then helped me and in some ways I think that has helped me in the future that I had to work more independently and take advice from different people and balance these things.

Certainly, these novice supervisors were close enough to being students to remember how hard it could feel on occasions. However, the key factor that linked all these novice supervisors was that, whatever difficulties they had faced, they had all completed their PhDs and had successfully started on academic careers. Some had already started on their academic careers while working on their PhDs, and this enabled them to find alternative supervisors and, possibly, to learn to read social and power dimensions of the situation more accurately.

Self-doubt: learning from others

In Chapter 6 we saw that new supervisors were slightly more likely than experienced ones to suffer self-doubt over their supervision, and the novice questionnaire group gave some insight into what this means. Being allocated supervision at the start of a supervisory career means one is more likely to be supervising 'out of your comfort zone' in terms of subject matter plus having only limited involvement in selection of students. So, while approaching supervision positively, it was, unsurprisingly, tinged with anxiety. Half agreed that *'supervising research students is a worry to me'*: *'Am I "good" enough?'*; *'Not being able to guide students to completion'*; *'Failing the student by not providing a suitable environment and amount of support for their development.'*

Concerns are not new or confined to the UK. McMichael (1993) described how new supervisors of postgraduate dissertations in Sri Lanka and Australia doubted aspects of their competence and were nervous of the time commitment required. In my group, self-doubt was similarly linked to subject knowledge plus time – the latter becoming an important issue where they are not supervising within their main area of expertise: *'Lack of in-depth knowledge of the subject matter. Admin workload'* and *'Having sufficient time – being pressured to take on students that I feel inappropriately qualified to supervise.'* One interviewee describes the process of working through worry to a level of confidence:

> I think I was really worried at the start, really worried that they [the students] were all doing lots of different areas, things I knew nothing about . . . We do think they are going to realize I am a fraud at some point; they will know that and that will be really embarrassing. I think because they are all very different and all doing very different things that I do think it is enjoyable.

In this case, the worry was part of the wider task of building up a firm professional confidence and belief in her academic identity.

One route to building up confidence is by working jointly or in teams with other supervisors, or in observing other supervisors at close quarters. One commented on joint supervision:

> I think my confidence is purely based on the fact that I am doing it with somebody else who I really trust. I don't know if I could do if I was just on my own at the minute, or maybe I undersell myself, but I am much happier that I am doing it with someone that I really respect.

Trust is based on respecting the co-supervisor's academic reputation as well as liking how they handle supervision sessions.

One interviewee had been impressed by her partner's ex-supervisor, even though she was at some distance from the university concerned. She had been impressed by how the supervisor both managed relationships and boundaries, although she thought she *'probably goes too far into the maternal role because that is how she is as a person'*. While she could see the faults in this approach, she had drawn from it that getting to know students mattered:

> It is a stereotype I suppose in that her door is always open, phone numbers are exchanged, home phone numbers, emails, she is lovely but I think there needs to be a boundary. I really like the way she is very welcoming and she has always made herself very open to students and will get to know them and their situations and families and things like that.

As well as getting to know students individually, she tried to form a community by bringing her students and their partners together:

> . . . and that was a really nice thing to do, bringing people together, and I've thought actually I'd really like to do that. It wasn't necessarily that she wanted to become friends with us all, but she was being friendly with us and saying 'we're all together'.

This interviewee was well aware of the dangers for herself, as a young woman starting out, of being seen as a source of pastoral care rather than as a serious academic. Her partner's ex-supervisor, she felt, was so outstandingly successful that her humanity added to her reputation rather than lessened it, setting an ideal for her to work towards: *'I think she has got quite a nice balance in some way with authority and gravitas and respect but also a humanness as well.'*

These responses can be conceptualized as indicating that novice supervisors have successfully become socialized into the dispositions of research (travelling through the stages from junior to senior researcher as in Hakala's model) or as having started on an academic career while finishing the PhD (akin to Amundsen and McAlpine's view of becoming a supervisor as part of the journey towards establishing an academic identity). In either case, they made use of informal and formal opportunities for observing supervision: as joint supervisors, their own varied experience of supervision, plus that of partners and colleagues. This gives a rich reservoir of experience to draw on for those who are able to reflect constructively and to evaluate experience creatively and potentially shapes what they hope for from becoming supervisors themselves.

Expectations of supervision

Two comments illustrate opposed views of supervision. One indicates the view that supervision is a sign of having achieved a certain status within an academic career: *'Excited but scared – new part of my academic journey!'* Whereas the second echoes the view that supervision is an allocated task over which one has little control, albeit a task that leads to career progression: *'It was imposed upon me – little/no choice – is seen as part of the promotion process to supervise.'* However, most novice questionnaire respondents anticipated supervision in a positive way: 85 per cent agreed that they welcome supervising research students (only two disagreed); 95 per cent agreed that they enjoy contact with research students; 65 per cent saw supervision as one of the rewards of the job (two did not, and five were unsure); all agreed that supervision is time-consuming, apart from two who were not sure; and all, bar one (who was unsure), saw supervision as challenging.

What this group most looked forward to in supervision was a combination of fostering another person's development coupled with involvement in novel, interesting work which maintained the supervisor's engagement with research. Establishing a good teaching relationship was fundamental to engaging in their preferred mode of supervision: *'Building a relationship with another and hopefully influencing them positively'*; *'Sitting down and discussing plans – completion (successful!)'*; and *'Being stretched and stimulated. Hopefully developing rewarding relationships (I probably have rose-tinted glasses on here).'* To see students develop was paramount: *'Seeing students develop and achieve professionally'*; *'To see students developing and learning'*; and *'Observing a student grow into an independent researcher.'* Vilkinas has commented that watching 'students grow and develop and doing research with them as colleagues were the most enjoyable aspects of the supervision process' (p. 297) for faculty members in her study; and this narrative was claimed in anticipation by this group of novice supervisors. This anticipated enjoyment of observed development included working with good students, *'having challenging/exciting and enthusiastic students to work with'*.

Echoing Amundsen and McAlpine's belief that starting to supervise is a part of developing an academic identity, the notion of a collaborative relationship was expressly linked to the novice supervisor's own continuing research identity and intellectual development through the students' work: *'Sharing students' developments; reading good work; seeing the thesis develop'*; *'Being involved in interesting research. Developing a collaborative research relationship with the student'*; and *'Teaching/working at a higher level – helping someone develop a research career – reading new material myself (or rereading theoretical work).'*

The supervisor's continuing intellectual development is, as we have seen already, about engagement in research through teaching, and through novel ideas: *'To see the student develop his ideas. This will give me time to think about research during a week which is otherwise often very busy with teaching and admin'*; *'Learning about a new topic. Sharing ideas/knowledge through collaboratively discussing ideas, problems . . .'*; *'Seeing my student evolve and progress. Opportunity to develop understanding in a specific area of research'*; and simply, *'New students, new perspectives.'* In short, supervision is anticipated with excitement as part of continuing to develop through knowledge and understanding of their subject area.

Implications for supervision

- New supervisors do not arrive at their first supervisions with identical levels of expertise. Most have a range of skills and experiences that relate to research and supervision. They have often taught, worked in research and research teams both during their own higher degrees and beyond. Designing a supervisor development course for such diversity of needs and knowledge is challenging. In addition, supervision training courses represent a number of agendas beyond those of the supervisor alone – including those of the institution and external bodies.

- New supervisors are much more likely to be inducted into supervision via courses, supervisory teams and mentoring than their more experienced colleagues were. However, translating institutional policies and codes into practice is not always easy to do on the ground, and novice supervisors remain likely to start their supervisory careers in complex situations: coming late to teams where key decisions have already been taken; coming after the loss of perhaps valued supervisors; or where relationships had become fractured.

- New supervisors' personal experience of PhD completion provides a reservoir of good and bad examples of supervision to call on in the early stages of supervisory careers. Like the completers in Chapter 3, new supervisors in this project had overcome real personal and intellectual challenges. The danger of this is a temptation to become too rigid in stating what supervision should be (although a number illustrated how responsive they were learning to be with each student). Heroic accounts follow completion, and perhaps partial socialization into the practices and dispositions of academe might have enabled access to solutions not obvious or available to other doctoral students.
- Supervision is a legitimate focus for worry: will I give the right advice, can I find students the right problems, will I find the right examiner? However, it is also a part of early-stage academics finding their way in a competitive, hierarchical world. Concerns about time, competency and authority experienced by this group of novice supervisors were shared over time and around the world (see Amundsen & McAlpine and McMichael for comparisons). Mentoring new supervisors needs to be embedded into wider systems for ensuring new academics are supported in their general adjustments to successful working in academe.

Novice supervisors bring with them the richness of what they have learned already and the qualities that have enabled their success to date. Individuals vary hugely in the uses they make of experience and vary in the social, personal and intellectual skills they bring to supervision. Each generation adjusts to their broad academic culture within a changing landscape of external demands – as disciplinary gatekeepers and guardians of standards, from governments and funders and from their employers. Supervision sits within this framework of complex demands, and novice supervisors must establish their identities as academics and researchers within a competitive working environment.

8 The Voice of Experience

Chapter Outline

Twelve experienced academics were recommended to me as outstanding supervisors. This chapter discusses four elements that recurred across my interviews with them: the notion of combining responsiveness to individual students with a knowledge of pathways through the PhD; a preference for a collegial, mentoring style of supervision in which they work alongside the student; an understanding of the place of critical evaluation in constructing academic knowledge, yet recognition of the difficulties in the supervisor's role as critic to their students; and experience of what can go wrong, from their perspective, in unsuccessful supervisions.

There can be clear advantages for students in working with academics experienced in supervision. They are probably experienced examiners and reviewers, usually having established their own research reputations and perhaps able to enjoy the successes of others while having developed a range of social skills over time. Of course, the disadvantages are that those who are successful researchers are likely to have only limited time as they bid for grants, run projects, supervise numerous students, take on roles with administrative responsibility, maintain their international reputation by visiting universities abroad, publishing and attending conferences as well as teaching and examining in their home universities. Their time may well be further taken up with national and international committees and advisory groups. There are disadvantages in working with those who are experienced but less successful supervisors, and as people grow in experience they do not all appreciate youthful enthusiasm or deviations from what they see as the set paths of research and writing. Not everyone grows in patience and social skills with age, and their insight into why students struggle with the PhD may become eroded over time.

My group of 12 experienced interviewees were all recommended to me as outstanding by people who knew their work – students, administrators, colleagues. Given that my project aims included developing teaching materials, it made sense to try to talk to experienced supervisors acknowledged by others to be good at the role. Experienced, in this case, was anyone who had seen more than three students through to successful completion either singly or jointly. Subject matter ranged through arts, social science and science subjects (both applied and pure studies). A number had seen 17, 20 or more through to completion (those teaching on doctoral programmes had often supervised even large numbers). I did not check out systematically the criteria by which they were judged to be outstanding, although reasons volunteered included high rates of student completion, sympathetic to students and even, on occasions, inspirational. Indeed, I remembered the inspiring quality described to me as I walked away at the end of one interview. I found myself trying to work out if I could perhaps do a part-time Master's course in this person's subject. Now one thing I do not need is another course in anything, so why this line of thinking? The interviewee was quite contained, a passion for the subject expressed and clearly present, but not overwhelming. Somehow they managed to speak with commitment and clarity, but in a way that allowed me space to see how the subject related to me – indeed, to catch fire in me.

Supervision is a complex relationship that is mediated through subject matter; calling on high-level communication and organizational skills over long periods of time; and positioned within international reference groups while framed by local teaching and management policies and practices. An adept supervisor needs to juggle all of these, and to do so at a time when universities are recruiting greater numbers of doctoral students. At heart, a PhD is a risky activity, taking both student and supervisor to the boundaries of their knowledge and capability, without any guarantees as to how they will cope in such a vulnerable zone. What, then, did these reportedly good supervisors bring to this pedagogic challenge? Overall, they shared an expectation that students would work towards independence as researchers, but this was combined with a range of approaches, interactions and strategies they had developed over time to support student progress.

What follows discusses (1) their use of both a responsive approach to students coupled with a sense of the best paths through the PhD in a mode I describe as 'flexi-structures'; and (2) their preference for a collegial, mentoring relationship in which they work alongside a student travelling towards autonomy and independence as a researcher. Feedback on student work and the role of critical evaluation in constructing academic knowledge are easily mistaken for each other in academic work plus students often find the process of receiving criticism difficult, so (3) I explore how reportedly good supervisors managed the process of feeding criticism back to students; and, finally, (4) I explore these supervisors' view of PhDs that appear to have gone wrong.

Flexi-structures

This group of experienced supervisors expressed awareness of pathways through the PhD from start to finish. Supervisors could call on a body of experience to compare current students' progress with those who had gone before. Having both a clear sense of the path to be travelled, coupled with awareness of their own supervisory style could, from one perspective, make this group sound rigid in the structures they believed were needed for successful PhDs. However, their descriptions of their supervisory styles were similar to that of Whitelock *et al.*'s social science supervisors in seeing the work as developmental and a 'subtle pedagogical practice that needs to be carefully tailored to students' developmental needs' (p. 147). Across disciplines, within this group of interviewees many expressed the belief that they were responsive to the needs of each student and each project, or at least tried to be. This combination of flexibility and clear structures is what I refer to as 'flexi-structures'. The intermingling of getting to know students well with progression through stages in the doctoral process were described by one social science supervisor, starting with assessing the nature of students' motivation.

> The first stage is kind of before they start, I always encourage them to come and see me . . . to try and get a sense of their motivation . . . It is great to have a good idea at the beginning, what you want to do, but that is no good unless they really want to do it, and so that's where it starts.

This supervisor was one of five in this group working with students whose professional work lies outside universities (e.g. justice system, health and others carrying out research in their workplaces) so arranging to attend these early meetings is not straightforward. Motivation, he felt, was especially essential for students to manage the 'deconstruction' experience of the first year, in which *'they have to throw everything out of the window and take everything to bits'*.

The next stage in his field of study was usually data collection, often in the student's area of professional expertise. But this, while usually enjoyable for students, leads to new problems with data – learning to analyse, manage and simplify the large amounts of data gathered. While the stages are clear, they do not follow neatly or take the same lengths of time for each study:

> As they move through the stages if you can see them leave one stage behind and enter another stage, you can start to get a good idea whether they are going to finish. But of course those stages . . . don't always take a nice year, one year, two years, three years for a full-time student, and sometimes they do it back to front, and that's really scary as well.

Given the numbers of part-time students working in their professional field, he was conscious of the need to align his supervisory style both to the demands of their lives, as well as the stage in the doctoral pathway:

> I try not to get worked up about deadlines, most of my students tend to be mature as well so I tend to want to listen to their, the way they pace themselves, try to get a sense of how they like to work and sort of work with that ... and then I sort of get quite hands-on towards the end and I'm at them all the time just before they submit,

One arts supervisor had seen many students through to successful completion, and was highly conscious of the variation in students, but matched this to her experience of the path generally travelled by past students. So, like the social science supervisor's notion of 'deconstruction' in Year 1, this supervisor regularly saw students go through a crisis in the early stages of Year 2:

> As a supervisor you've got to be very, very open minded, because sometimes you can have a student that starts off poorly and it would be easy to write them off, but they come through. Other ones hit the ceiling fairly soon and don't develop, so you've got learn all sorts of flexibilities . . . most students will have some kind of crisis with their project and that is normally, if they're a full time, at the end of the second year. I've seen enough of it now to be able to predict when things are likely to happen, which I now share with students . . .

These comments illustrate the difficulties attached to a common assumption that 'problem' students should be identified early in their first year and decisions then made about their suitability for doctoral education.

Students of one applied science lecturer were also mainly engaged in professional careers outside universities and he was concerned that students' social skills should develop over the course of the PhD as a basis for future consultancy work. He combined this broader education with ensuring opportunities to get to know his students well, so that he could tailor his supervisory behaviour accordingly. Of his full-time students, he said:

> I have a formal weekly timetable slot for everybody I supervise, so that they know that I am available then and I always tell them if it is only for you to put your head around the door and say you are fine, but I do want to see you every week. In practice it usually is much more than that, and I also say that I am available at other times but they have to make appointments . . . but as much as possible I make myself available at morning coffee, and I encourage my students and my RAs [research assistants] to come and just chat about the weather or whatever, but sometimes we get into work conversations there.

Conversations go beyond keeping in touch and include developing a 'social' dimension to research that extends to learning to network, borrowing ideas and engaging with training:

> I encourage them to talk to each other and to see themselves as part of a group rather than an individual, and try to arrange that they can travel to some extent within financial limits to meetings . . . I try to get them all to understand that their thesis topics sits within the wider context of . . . a discipline, so that minimally I want all my supervisees to end up as competent professionals . . . rather than someone who knows everything there is to know about their topic. So it is a kind of an attempt to bring them into a community of . . . colleagues with their own particular research project within that.

Using this combination of knowledge of the student, knowledge of the PhD pathway and his substantial success in the subject area the supervisor acted as an effective gatekeeper for his students. This approach encompasses a particular view of what a successful PhD student looks like: he encouraged them to understand their place in a wider professional world, which required communication skills rather than to become lone researchers, however knowledgeable.

Collaborative supervision

This group of supervisors had a picture in their head of the nature of relationship they preferred to set up with research students. Akin to the mentoring tutorship described in Chapter 1, another term that recurred was 'collegial'. Elton and Pope (1989) have associated collegial practices with underlying organizational structures that contain limited hierarchies (so, they associate collegial practices less with science teams). Educationally, the mutuality of a collegial style recognizes students' qualities and fosters dispositions such as autonomy and independence in researchers. However, the current prevalence of review panels and progression management systems in all subjects must make collegiality harder to achieve if Elton and Pope's thesis holds true. What follows indicates that 'collegial' is perhaps a goal of research education, similar to the academic dispositions of independence and robustness in defence of one's thesis, rather an absolute presence throughout. What level of collegiality is possible may depend on context and the people concerned and will vary at different stages in the doctoral journey. The journey starts in supervisors enjoying research students' work and respecting them as fellow researchers.

An appreciation of what students brought to supervision was predicated, for some supervisors, on their own success and commitment to their discipline which allowed them an enjoyment of student achievement. For the applied scientist, enjoyment of student success was tied up with a sense of responsibility for the future of his subject, whose applications are not confined to universities alone:

> It's working with enthusiastic, well-motivated people and feeling that you're actually helping them develop their careers and it is also, in my case, a very, very strong commitment to the fact that I think the discipline that I supervise in is both important and a scarcity area. There aren't enough well-trained people in it, so I actually think it is very important for the future health of the discipline and its application.

Like the applied scientist, one social scientist had been an early proponent of doctoral programmes for professionals who will apply their work in the field rather than become academics. But his enjoyment of supervision will be recognizable to many who do not teach doctoral PhDs:

> The enjoyable bits are students come up with things you haven't been aware of, ideas, publications, they do what you suggest sometimes, they do it well, they pass, they go on and have careers, they remember you.

One social science supervisor described the enjoyment of watching new students take their particular subject matter and develop it to a level of knowledge that could never be attained by the supervisor.

> It is a sort of trajectory and watching that trajectory and people obviously going off and giving their first talks, papers, conferences and all that sort of thing. So all that is very interesting and plus . . . people connecting with other people, other academics. So one nice thing was this book . . . and most of those chapters were done by my own research students at different times.

Respect for students' work arises out of mutuality, in which both gain. So, as well as the satisfaction of knowing that their supervision has contributed to the regeneration of the discipline itself, good supervision brings the supervisor satisfaction through extending their own, personal understanding and knowledge of the student's topic. Echoing the new supervisors' aspirations for supervision, an arts supervisor described the intellectual stimulation that comes with enthusiastic students:

> I've always found their enthusiasms provoke my enthusiasm, prompt them. I just find them very stimulating company but it is . . . often starting with a broad area of interest, and then just seeing how they work it down to something quite specific and I've found myself actually just being sucked in to their topic area and I kind of think 'I wish I was doing this', that kind of sensation, just the pleasures of their discovery of the ideas around the material.

This, then, can lead to a form of teaching which is more iterative and interactive than didactic in the traditional sense of imparting the supervisor's subject knowledge:

> If it works well it is not actually like teaching it is conversation, and therefore it is a kind of process of becoming informed and I'm very well aware that a good deal of my own research and of teaching other students at undergraduate level has been informed by listening to bright people who have been doing primary research.

This conversational style of mentoring and tutoring requires students to take responsibility for their work, albeit within the flexi-structures of an experienced supervisors' sense of what the optimum pathway through a PhD might be. These interactive, dynamic relationships are easiest to achieve with full-time students who are accommodated close to where their supervisor works. However, some of this group were applying a similar model to students studying part time, at a distance and on professional-based PhD programmes where it is harder to reproduce the conditions in which they can get to know students well. These other modes of doctoral study require particular sorts of exchanges to establish a working understanding early in a student's doctoral registration and need to be followed up throughout registration.

Learning to accept criticism

A traditional form of knowledge construction is the process of questioning, analysing, defending and reforming analysis that underpins much research activity. Evaluating evidence and sifting data is a key element in this process. In addition to this tradition of critical appraisal, the process of taking a PhD forward also casts the supervisor in the role of critic, responding analytically to students' work. These two strands of critical response can be mistaken for one another, and there are times when students feel unable to produce any more work as they disappear into what can feel like a mire of unfavourable criticism. In contrast to a critical approach, Whitelock *et al.* argue that in collaborative relationships, 'positive regard, established trust, mutual under-standing and shared goals' are part of what enables creative risk-taking in students (p. 151). So when attempting to gain insight into the supervisory strategies used by this group, I asked: how do your students learn to manage criticism?

An applied science supervisor recognized the inherent difficulty of giving critical feedback but also saw it as fundamental to how researchers develop understanding of a subject. He argued that successful researchers need to engage in self-criticism to achieve clarity and logic, to evaluate the worth of their own evidence before presenting it in a public arena. He recognized the public nature of criticism and the need for personal robustness on the part of students, hence a need for engagement in developing appropriate academic dispositions around critical questioning both in supervision sessions and elsewhere:

> I always strongly encourage my students to give talks, even the shy ones and I know they respond very badly to ill-thought-out critical remarks from the audience, and I try to make light of it. 'Oh yes I'm in a bad mood today!' or 'I don't really mean this'. I try to get them to be a little bit more robust, but at the same time I think it is very important that when you do criticize a student, you do it in a way that sees merit in what they are doing and offers a new direction, rather than just saying 'this is rubbish'. But to some extent it is part of academic give-and-take that you have to be robust to criticism. As long as the criticism isn't personal and isn't vicious, you have to learn to handle it.

A social scientist similarly encouraged students to understand that criticism is fundamental to academic endeavour, as a strategy to engage students with feedback as a method, not as a personal attack. In part, this approach emerged because she was aware of her own learning curve in response to critical feedback:

> I think none of us like criticism. I mean, even from sending an article for peer review and it comes back and you think, 'oh this is unfair', we just don't like it. I'm now really to the extent of saying, 'well if that is what the peer reviewer wants, that is what the peer reviewer is going to get', and I don't worry about it anymore, but I still worry about book reviews of my books.

Hence, she felt explaining the role of feedback was part of a processual commentary that accompanies engagement with the student's topic of research. This approach requires supervisors to work with students to deconstruct the dynamics of what is happening within supervision, alongside engagement with the research itself. For example, she explained that feedback is a problem:

> . . . but I always address this right up front with a student and say, 'when you come to a supervision session and you've given me work beforehand I'm going to criticize it because that is my job, but at the end of the day it is your thesis it is not mine, so you can either accept or reject my criticism'. Hopefully they will see this as constructive rather than trying to put them down. I've never had that problem where students get upset by it, even with very good students. I think very good students would probably feel they're getting shoddy service if I said 'oh yes this is fine', then they would begin to 'think has she read it?'

For this supervisor, managing criticism is a key part of helping students to negotiate the journey towards becoming independent researchers by internalizing the iterative, questioning process, both with external evidence and with their own work:

> Because I think you've got to get the student to think critically about his or her own work and if in the early stages you can say, 'you've stated this but where is your evidence for it?' or 'you've got in support, you have got the author of an article or book, do you agree with this person?'

To one social science supervisor, giving feedback on the first written piece was an opportunity to learn about the students:

> I can't predict how each student is going to react to having my comments. So that
> first time, when I give them comments on something that they've produced and
> it nearly always is a piece of written work, I am sort of watching and gauging,
> how are they responding to this? Because some students find it really difficult to
> handle anything that could be perceived as negative, and other students quite like
> it and like to argue things . . . You don't feed back in the same way to every stu-
> dent because they react differently to different kinds of comments.

The student's response is fundamental to the pedagogic dilemma faced by
supervisors: how to maintain students' energy and enthusiasm while providing criticism of the work? A robust student who can take criticism in good
part will probably advance more quickly than one who is easily upset. But for
this social science supervisor, that knowledge did not excuse unthinking
behaviour or unkindness which she recognized did exist and felt needed to
be tackled head-on in colleagues. Another social scientist did not like the
vocabulary of 'critical feedback', because of the unpleasant tone and nature of
some of the knock-about negativity that can be experienced in conferences
and presentations. Rather, he preferred to use a collegial, relaxed style of conversation as a framework for introducing criticism:

> . . . maybe the way I talk to them about it is to say 'I need to say things to you
> that somebody in the back of the audience at this conference might ask you, and
> you have no idea who they are, where they are coming from, but this is the kind
> of thing that might happen, so what would your answer be?' Kind of being a
> Devil's Advocate. I would say that the way that I try and move students thinking
> forward is more by engaging in quite an intense conversation with them about it,
> where we are both actually trying to puzzle out where is this thing's going and
> what other really important issues are in this.

Criticality, for this supervisor, indicated an unconstructive approach, whereas
deconstruction was about 'pushing people's thinking' and 'trying to get behind
peoples' assumptions. In explaining an unconstructive approach to criticism,
he gave insight into the problems for social science students attached to
competing paradigms:

> I suppose my experience of that kind of criticism or debate is often people who
> are kind of passing each other by. The strongest examples of that I've been
> involved with are really where we have got different paradigms arguing with each
> other in the same room and it can be very damaging and, in the context of PhD
> study, it is not particularly helpful because you are trying to build an argument,

> you are trying to move toward some shared understanding of an issue. Whereas those sorts of debates are often just 'I'm going there, and you're going there, I don't like what you do so I'm going tell you!'

Working with a written text allowed this supervisor to keep to a collegial conversation, but he was less able to manage this tenor of discussion when working orally. Written work allows him the opportunity to prepare responses to the content of the text, but also to prepare mentally for the conduct of a supervision session.

When it goes wrong

All supervisors (good or bad, novice or experienced) will meet, at some point, with a student who does not complete or who finds the PhD too uncomfortable to derive any level of satisfaction. Few supervisors in this group were untouched by their 'failures', and some had been profoundly shaken by examples of supervision that were less than they had hoped for. However, not all of these had resulted in student withdrawal without PhDs, many had graduated successfully.

I asked one scientist to describe how they began to recognize when a PhD problem was moving from being a problem to something bigger. The answer made it plain that their sense of the pathways through the doctoral process was part of what made such a judgement possible:

> I suppose it is when the student somehow doesn't seem to be able to get, not only ownership of the problem, but the ability to identify and solve the problems that they are encountering for themselves because I don't mind at the beginning of the process giving them quite a lot of help with understanding things and just getting things right, but if that process keeps on going on then I start getting alarmed because I feel as though the student ought to be able to manage without such detailed input.

The pathway from dependent student to autonomous researcher was a progression in understanding and was clear to this supervisor; and it was assessed through a student's expression of research behaviour, yet was described as a set of personal characteristics that the student needed to display. Both sides are likely to lose faith in each other: if the student does not share the cultural references by which to make sense of the path they are being ushered along; if they cannot intellectually make the transition; or if the student does not share the supervisor's expectation of increased independence.

In this particular case, the nature of the subject matter is such that undergraduate and Master's courses are unlikely to have provided new PGR students fully with the skills needed for the PhD, so there is an expectation on the supervisor's part that the initial stages include a level of direct tutoring coupled with the student being able to contribute directly themselves to bridging that gap:

> I ought to explain that the field I'm working in is fairly specialized, and there are problems about gaps between undergraduate knowledge and the knowledge that they need to do the sort of things that we do . . . we've got some postgraduate courses which they can take which can plug some of the gaps, but it does depend a bit on what the student has done as an undergraduate . . . So some of this is actually about trying to arrange the students who can bridge that gap and get to the point where they understand enough to be able to move forward without so much detailed help.

In this subject area, then, the new student must be able to take initiative and work courageously with new material.

Striving for intellectual autonomy may be assumed to be unnecessary for science students working in teams and laboratory work by comparison with social science or arts students. However, the following scientist made it clear that a similar intertwining of personal characteristics with research understanding was the locus of problems when the PhD was going wrong. She had jointly supervised a student, and both supervisors found themselves unable to communicate successfully with him about some of the basics of what constitute meaningful results and she concluded that as a supervisor:

> The worries come where there is a lack of fit between the . . . idealized model and everybody being able to play their part in it and the student who for one reason or another, there are always lots of different reasons when there are problems, are not able to live up to that. Then the worries come about and what do you do about that?

The recognition that problems are, as in this specific case, going to be insurmountable can dawn slowly, not least because other students may well have succeeded in similar circumstances:

> I have mostly been lucky that people that I have supervised, they have mostly been highly competent even if not in the things that we have wanted to do, but not always. When there is a breakdown . . . it is not usually deeply fundamental, it is something which nevertheless may lead to the student withdrawing. Yes there is

> a point at which where, in an instant, problem cases, it gradually grows on you.
> I think I do have, without having it usually written out, a scheme through which
> I expect we work, a pace at which I expect to be moving and so on. The farther
> that you fall away from that the more uncomfortable [you become].

Paradoxically, while full recognition of the impact of problems might grow over time, she also felt that the first feelings of doubt arise early on:

> Where I have had serious problems with students I have usually recognized there
> is going to be a problem here within the first six months certainly, shorter than
> that often. It hasn't always continued seriously, but it is usually fairly early on that
> you sort of think 'uh oh this is not going to be one of those fully rewarding experi-
> ences throughout the three years'.

The difficulty being, as she expressed, that the problems may be surmountable even if the supervisory experience is not rewarding, or they may not prove to be surmountable in the end. Experience, in this case, showed her that perseverance can result in unpromising students' successful completion of a thesis.

One social science supervisor was similarly clear that growing recognition that problems will impact detrimentally on a thesis has a slow trajectory over time. Students, in his view, follow a path from hesitancy and dependency in the first months to becoming independent and responsible researchers. The most frustrating students, for him, are those who could not make the transition to autonomous researcher. His preferred supervisory style was to be accessible and to work in a collegial, mentoring relationship with students, modelling what was expected of them as researchers:

> My supervisory style would try to relate to the particular person, so it would be
> adjusted to the person and therefore you have to be a goodish analyst at what
> is going to work for somebody, and that among other things the mixture of
> friendliness and formality, rule following or being fair about what has to be done
> at what sorts of times. Also leading by example, so I often give them copies of
> things I've written. I like it best when it turns into a collegial situation, which
> works fine with some people and then they see things which you've written
> which hopefully inspires them to write something vaguely similar.

With the majority of his students, this style had enabled progress towards autonomy, but he had met some for whom this had not worked:

> The quicker it moves into a collegial situation the better, but of course there
> are annoying people . . . you are more leading people by the hand. I am quite

> unsympathetic to people who are in their third or fourth years, are still asking
> you the things, not trying to think and that as such, particularly . . . one who . . .
> I thought the problem was he had not grown up sufficiently to take responsibility.
> This was his thesis, he had to figure out how much had to be done and the length
> of the literature and the amount of data he should have been collecting.

While the problems manifested themselves in dependent behaviour around the research, the supervisor experienced it as a matter of the student's personal characteristics. It is not clear whether or not the expectations of this level of independence were implicit or made explicit. The student, however, had not progressed to knowing *how* to take research decisions confidently and this was experienced by the supervisor as a deficiency in the student's character.

In all these cases, fundamental communication about what was expected of researchers was unsuccessful. The supervision process had been experienced by the supervisors as unsatisfactory and the students had not conformed to the pathway in the supervisors' heads in negotiating key developmental tasks and displaying desired academic dispositions on route to doctorateness. However, the students were still (mainly) successful at some sort of level – not all left with uncompleted theses. This, of itself, illuminates the dilemma: when getting early 'bad' feelings, successful supervisors' experience may well show that this is no indicator of who will succeed or not at the end, and that the trajectory for such decisions to be reasonable and fair may well be a long one. Further, people who successfully negotiate key developments connected to the early stages of a PhD may not necessarily manage the challenges associated with the final stages.

Implications for supervision

- The importance of responsiveness to the needs of individual students was high on the list for these supervisors (although we have no information about how students experienced this). It combined with awareness of stages and pathways through the PhD. While some of these supervisors had pioneered doctoral programmes, recruited students who study part time or at a distance, responsiveness to individual students is most easily achieved when students work within the university. Extra effort is needed to sustain a similar sort of relationship when students are not full time or do not study nearby, along with the use of Skype, blogs, emails and proper management of those meetings which do take place.
- The preferred style for many was a collegial, mentoring relationship in which they gave students opportunities to travel along the continuum from new student to independent researcher. This implies an agreed sense (or growing awareness) of

Implications for supervision—Cont'd

the division of responsibility for and ownership of the PhD, which may not be present in all supervisory relationships. When student and supervisors privately hold different views, then if the PhD goes wrong there is room for great frustration on both sides. Many institutions now provide workshops and courses which help students to reflect on the processes and goals involved in doing a PhD and attendance at these can ease supervisory relationships.

- Criticality as a method and critical feedback on work can become intertwined in a PhD, which can rapidly turn research from a constructive process into one in which the student feels undermined. Careless and repeated critical feedback over time within a culture of deconstructing everyone else's work is not creative or encouraging. The challenge for supervisors is to provide criticism, maintain student enthusiasm and encourage evaluative, critical engagement with the discipline without sinking into destructive and dispiriting habits.

- All supervisors, at some point, will meet students who do not finish their PhDs for a wide variety of reasons. Given that the PhD is challenging throughout, and that not every student develops at the same pace, the trajectory towards withdrawal is not as clear-cut when current as it is in retrospect. Not all who find the first year easy necessarily manage the final stages, so early withdrawal does not always offer the desired solutions. However, supervisors need to be aware that funding bodies increasingly expect students who have progressed beyond Year 1 to finish a PhD successfully within a set period. Paradoxically, experience of successful supervision may contribute to a reluctance to call 'time' on an unpromising student too early, knowing that others have still managed to finish successfully.

As an interviewer, I found these interviews (mainly) enjoyable. This stood in marked contrast to how 'experienced supervisors' figured throughout the rest of the project: colleagues' descriptions saw experienced supervisors as slow to change and resistant to training and new ways of doing things. Interviewees had been recommended as good supervisors, so unsurprisingly usually had good social skills, enjoyed their students, were successful researchers, innovative teachers (through doctoral programmes and in working with professionals in their allied fields) and had a commitment to the development of their disciplines. As a group, they had evidently thought carefully about supervision.

The clarity and immediacy of answers reflected the time they had spent (over years) reflecting on supervisory meetings and on student progress. What was less clear and would require different information is whether there were patterns to which students could not easily make the transition to the expected levels of autonomy or how misunderstandings about the allocation of respon-sibility for success are experienced by struggling students. The challenges for this group lay in adjusting to tighter timelines, given their prior experience that unpromising students can succeed and in transferring responsiveness to individual students into an environment where many students will be part time and working at a distance. Further, while most of their students had suc-ceeded, it is not clear from these accounts how to proceed with students who, in the final stages, cannot attain the key academic disposition of researcher independence or who do not share the same sense of where responsibility for student academic success lies.

Part 4
Development and Training

Training courses and development activities for supervisors have become more common in universities in recent years. But they have received a mixed response from supervisors themselves, who recognize that supervisory skills are derived from their experience and standing vis à vis a range of academic activities (e.g. research, scholarship, reviewing), and require mentoring rather than courses.

Academic managers in this study, however, had a clearer view of the functions and preferred style of training courses. All were agreed that new supervisors required training but experienced supervisors were perceived as resistant to change and to course attendance. Managers felt experienced supervisors needed to understand that the world had changed. However, responses to a national survey illustrated how many experienced supervisors have attended courses and are flexible in their understanding of supervision. Interviews, however, showed that some experienced supervisors were perplexed as to how a lifetime of research could be summarized and taught.

Meanwhile, course designers such as myself juggle pragmatism with complex pedagogic reflection, where supervisors are concerned with their specific research worlds. The supervisors' recognition that becoming a supervisor is a developmental process provided a forceful reminder of the power of experiential learning in teaching development.

Supervisor Courses: Training and Development 9

Looking back

The PhD has been presented throughout this book as high level, research education. Even though it now comes in many shapes and forms, all PhDs require a level of commitment from students who must focus on a chosen area of study over some years – whether full or part time. It provides excitement, for subjects chosen for dissertations are at the edge of a discipline's development, and it requires imagination and creativity, as well as accuracy, research skills and scholarship. It helps if students are good communicators: as writers, in presentations and teaching, and as negotiators. Certainly, there will be frequent opportunities to practise and develop in all these areas during doctoral work. Enjoying the chance to steep oneself in research and scholarship is essential, as is a willingness to enjoy overcoming intellectual challenges.

In my courses for students, it is clear that people are better at some parts of this than others and manage challenges differently at different points in their lives. There is a transformational element to research education: it is not enough just to tick boxes and 'acquire' skills, rather intellectual challenge can overturn students' existing understanding and ways of looking at work, in order to produce new answers. Intellectually, the path may represent risk. It is one of the reasons that frustration levels can be so high on occasions, for a researcher may have a sense of where they want to get to but cannot yet see a route from here to there. Hence, hitting low points can be particularly exasperating. In my tutorials, groups and courses with students I am now far more confident in understanding the place of 'play' in doctoral education: talking with other students, accepting frustration as a sign that there is a key to progress (not a barrier) in the offing, experimenting with writing and allowing time to enrich understanding. At one time I found work such as Cameron's *The Artist's Way* too removed from doctoral education (not least because I am uncomfortable with a spiritual notion of creativity, which I feel is produced by earth-bound human beings); however, now I recognize much more clearly that the pragmatic, box-ticking parts of the PhD only succeed when we combine them with working on how to negotiate tricky, creative challenges.

So, paradoxically, one of the doctoral challenges for students is to embrace frustration as part of a creative, transformational process yet within a self-disciplined framework. Transformation goes beyond the cognitive in what is needed for successfully meeting intellectual challenges, and includes personal and emotional changes in the socialization process that is the development of 'academic dispositions'. Planning projects, managing supervisors, forward-planning, developing research skills and understanding have to sit side-by-side with enjoyment of intellectual adventures. There is plenty of advice available on the web and in print for students, and many institutions run 'general' courses to help PGR students to develop key and transferable skills. But in the end, students have to learn how to take research decisions independently and how to enjoy academic independence. Learning to listen, to take advice, to understand and integrate it intelligently – learning when to go solo with decisions and when not – are essential lessons in the PhD.

One of the biggest challenges I face when working with students is to offer an alternative perspective from that of the detail of their study, to help people learn to step back and to see their research from a wider angle. The balance between commitment and obsession is a fine one. What starts as excitement and love of a topic can rapidly turn into a mass of detail that occupies the whole of a student's life. Supervisor and student can join each other together on what one of my interviewees called 'planet PhD', which allows little else of life in. As the completers in Chapter 3 showed us, obsession is necessary for completion but it needs to be balanced with openness to new ways of thinking, new ways of looking at problems and the possibility that new information can overturn existing understanding. Encouraging people to step back is part of finding ways to help students make the major transition in mindset from doctoral student to doctoral graduate.

Chapters 3 and 4 illustrated how students experience both good and bad in their doctoral education. But good and bad are rarely absolutes: each PhD is a highly personalized experience and what is a problem for one is an advantage to another (even something as apparently concrete as lack of funding). For the completers 'bad' experiences were part of a sense of heroically overcoming transformational ordeals and achieving success – so the sense of achievement would not have been the same had they not faced problems and solved them along the way. I have always seen individual's own solutions as the most valuable, however, I approach my courses and tutorials with much more confidence now that I see how supporting students in finding solutions supports a key endeavour in doctoral education, rather than giving into pressure to constantly offer solutions myself. Current students and completers illustrated the process of socialization into academic dispositions as learnt within their subject areas, and show the journey of adjustment from initial expectations to understanding the reality of research.

Balancing an institution's interests with those of supervisors and students was illustrated in Chapter 5 by looking at some 'hidden' supports in universities. Most of the interviewees were removed from direct involvement in supervision, and will be seen by students and supervisors to be complicit in producing policies and bureaucratic procedures complained of by others. It was clear, though, that this group felt no more sense of agency than supervisors and students did; plus their vantage points within institutions shaped what they saw as 'common sense' approaches, particularly to developing supervisory teams and supervisor training. They tended to talk of the PhD in clear, systemic ways that permit smooth progress; this is in contrast to writers such as Grant who emphasize the inherently messy nature of research.

Those who filled in my questionnaires and answered my questions were clearly committed to high standards in their work, both students and supervisors. In Chapter 6, supervisors talked about their concerns and the sense of responsibility they felt towards their students. From choice, supervisors preferred to work from well within their own subject area, feeling uncomfortable when pressured to supervise in an area less familiar to them. They enjoyed the intellectual challenge of working with bright and motivated students on problems at the edge of their disciplines – extending their own knowledge of specific areas while watching students outstrip them in understanding and moving onto successful careers (whether or not these were in academe). They feared most taking on students who turn out not to be able to make the transition to independent researchers. Both students and supervisors shared a narrative about the centrality of student characteristics (of resilience, perseverance and independence) in enabling student progression. What is not clear is when students develop this narrative, and how close it is to their expectations prior to arrival.

New supervisors turned out to be not so new after all. By the time they had reached training courses and first supervisions, most had travelled a rich and varied academic route. As well as their own experience of being PGR students, they had observed other supervisions via friends and partners, through joint supervisions, through taking part in departmental review panels and through working as post-docs in research teams. They had published their first articles (and books), attended conferences, given papers and reviewed journal articles. They tended, of course, to be up-to-date in their subject area and to have attended training courses on aspects of teaching in addition to supervision. What they lacked was integration of this range of experience and skills into the sort of confidence and authority that comes from having supervised sufficient numbers of PGR students to assess their own progress as supervisors.

Experienced supervisors were presented throughout my project as resistant to change and to training. The group interviewed were chosen because others had recommended them as good or successful as supervisors. Like all other supervisors who took part in this project, they showed clear enjoyment of the intellectual challenge of working with PGR students, especially those supervisors who saw themselves as contributing to the future health and shape of their subject area. They tended to view themselves as both responsive to individual students' styles and needs, yet contained this within the frame of an optimum pathway through the PhD as a process. Like supervisors in Chapter 6, supervisions that went wrong (which were not necessarily the same as students not graduating) were typified by finishing students not attaining the sorts of independence and autonomy expected in a doctoral researcher. Their experience of mentoring a range of students to graduation made it both harder and easier to pick up on problems: they recognized early when supervision was going to feel less rewarding, but had worked with a variety of students (and by implication, abilities) to help them finally achieve a successful thesis, making it harder to predict who would not manage the final hurdles.

My courses and group work with students have undergone steady change since the early 1980s, when I started to work with PGR students, and have been informed by generations of students and their feedback. The steady absorption of information over time has enabled me to develop ways of working, try out different approaches and reach a level of equilibrium between consolidation and change. This project started, however, because I did have the same sense of certainty about providing courses for supervisors. An individual NTFS award allowed me the opportunity to deconstruct my teaching and courses for supervisors of research students. So rather than being an exhaustive piece of research, this book represents my journey as I filtered what I knew, spoke to people inside universities, listened to their opinions and read their analyses of research education. In sharing my process of deconstruction, I have presented implications for supervision in the hopes that practitioners can borrow from this and adapt ideas for their own work. At the end of this particular journey, however, I needed to reconstruct my teaching and change or continue with my existing courses for supervisors.

In 2000, after many years of working with doctoral students in difficulties (often describing their problems with supervisors), I had started to provide short courses for supervisors. My hopes, originally, were probably naïve and partly lay in wanting to limit the numbers of students needing to request my help. However, I never intended (or believed) that courses could be the sole or best means of providing developmental work for supervisors. Supervision is too complex a job, in interpersonal fluency, in disciplinary engagement as well as in intellectual and pedagogic skills, for traditional courses. Plus, since I first started courses for supervisors we have moved through an era of what has been variously called the 'audit culture', the 'knowledge economy', the 'bureaucratization of higher education' and the 'massification of higher education'. The political and institutional context in which supervision occurs has changed substantially, and what seemed reasonable as a curriculum for supervisor courses in 2000 may no longer be so clear-cut today.

Now it is commonplace to assume that supervisors should attend training courses, even though experienced supervisors are believed to resist this, which was far from the case in 2000. That means that early attendees at my courses had chosen to attend, whereas now, in contrast, 'voluntary' attendance has overtones of 'well, I guess I have to sign up for this'. Getting to know one's constituencies is a basic rule for educational developers, so understanding the issues supervisors face and trying to find ways of influencing their academic practices has to be a keystone to good practice. This requires information. There are large amounts of information for trainers and developers to tap into in the course of their work: feedback forms; meetings with course participants; hearing the 'real' story directly from friends; working with students; listening to contributions in committees; teas, coffee, lunch breaks during courses; doing the same activities as course participants if possible or finding opportunities for shadowing parts of the work (e.g. examining, reviewing and supervising); quality of assignments when assessment is part of a course; detailed reflection when courses are finished; and reading the now large corpus of printed work on supervision.

Primary research is the option I chose on this occasion, combined with my experience drawn from many of the above. So, before finally considering how I may now reconstruct my teaching, I want to explore some information that I gathered to illustrate these supervisors' views of training and development work. I draw on the interviews with academic-managers, the national survey of supervisors and interviews with experienced staff to see what picture of training and development emerges.

Supervisors' views of training and development

Management interviews

In Chapter 5, we saw how supervisors with management roles sat between systemic understandings of supervision, and the highly individualized accounts of students and many supervisors. Only one of these interviewees had actually attended any kind of supervision course themselves. All saw the big challenge for training across the sector as lying with professional development for experienced supervisors. One summarized this:

> So the big challenge is to somehow help long-established supervisors to understand that actually the world has actually moved on since on they were in Cambridge in the 1970s, it doesn't work that way anymore.

Hence, one aspect to this professional development is 'procedural awareness' and engagement with regulations as they are currently. These changes were described as closely linked to assumptions about why students are doing a PhD in the first place and supervisors' expectations about developing the next generations of academics within their subject:

> I think it's about 30 percent of PhD students become academics, ergo 70 don't. and I think . . . it's part of a bigger shift in the PGR landscape from simply the output in terms of a thesis which most supervisors still cherish as what PhD work is about.

So for this interviewee, perceived resistance to training among experienced supervisors was part of needing to recognize how the world had changed, both procedurally and in students' purposes in registering for PhDs.

Academic managers had some clear ideas about how training should be carried out but saw no problems in assuming that the needs of the institution in providing courses would be identical with those of supervisors. Rather than courses alone, working alongside experienced supervisors was seen as essential yet, as one argued, what exactly one learns from experienced or principal supervisors in a team is not always best practice: '*Whether that means they simply learn the bad habits of the principle supervisor is another point*'.

However, mentoring and learning from others coupled with courses was a popular suggestion. But as well as being dependent on well-informed and up-to-date mentors (at odds with the notion that experienced supervisors are all out of step with current practice), it was recognized that there is an inherent danger in this system that 'second' supervisors are seen as trainee rather than encouraging genuinely joint supervisory teams. One interviewee felt, additionally, that this would lead to departmentally based training, which is too limited:

> I think that it must involve a range of staff young and old . . . Second thing I think you want to do is to very crucially ensure that whoever is teaching this is a range of people from a range of disciplines . . .

He went on to make explicit what he felt training meant to most academics:

> I think most academics have little patience with training that is done in the kind of ways that a lot of trainers want to do them, with breakout rooms and talk about this and talk round it. While we are quite sophisticated people when it comes to our research . . . we want black and white solutions here and anything that doesn't give us that is regarded as a waste of time. That may not be very mature of us, but it's the way we are.

For this interviewee, professional development was, ideally, about short delivery of clear statements about what the PhD and supervision is, ideally, backed by some authoritative statement from senior university management.

Survey responses

Responses to the first exploratory questionnaire I used with 15 supervisors reflected the view that learning to be a supervisor is a developmental, experiential process, one that had not solely been informed by being a research student, but was influenced by subsequent supervisory experience and, for some, by undergoing training of some sort. This was, similarly, the case in the national questionnaire. For example:

> I probably started from my experience as a research student. Then I have learnt from each student. I think it is very useful to have discussions with other people to help reflect on student supervision and whether there is anything I should be doing differently.

As a trainer, I have often been told that PGR supervision is too subject-specific to be amenable to general training, but most disagreed with this view. Indeed, as the next comment illustrates, those who had experienced training valued talking to a range of other supervisors:

> I was well supervised for my PhD, but recognized the style may not suit everyone. I wanted to know about options and styles in a broader context and was happy to see a course available. So I took the opportunity and was pleased to find many other 'experienced' supervisors also on the course.

As this comment illustrates, while there is a common belief that experienced staff resist courses, this is not longer entirely the case (and my courses have been attended by experienced supervisors during their ten years in existence).

As in the pilot work, responses to the national survey showed that supervisors see learning to be a supervisor as an experiential matter: 65 per cent agreed that they had learnt how to supervise from experience, while only 7 per cent disagreed; and 68 per cent agreed they had learnt from students they supervised. While acknowledging the experiential element in supervisor development, the group were divided over the statement 'training on the job is best for supervisors', with 43 per cent agreeing, 27 per cent disagreeing and over a quarter unable to say one way or the other. Just over 51 per cent of the questionnaire group of 108 had attended some kind of supervisor training course, and a little over 40 per cent said they had not. These courses ranged from one-off induction days to full, Master's-level modules carried out over extended time periods, with seminars and residential weekends in between. However, as one pointed out, separating formal training from development is not easy to do:

> It depends what you mean by training . . . I think I've learned from co-supervising and from talking to colleagues about supervision – I haven't had formal training

and I'm not certain how useful this would be, although perhaps I have been lucky in being able to talk to others.

50 per cent agreed that it is difficult to get staff to undergo formal supervisor training (31 per cent were not sure and 15 per cent disagreed). Only 3 per cent disagreed with the statement that established staff were more resistant to training than newer staff (61 per cent agreed and 32 per cent could not decide). 73 per cent agreed that all new supervisors should undergo training. When it came to the statement, 'PGR supervision is too subject-specific to provide general training for', a startling 61 per cent disagreed – in complete contrast to the view I have heard for many years that the PhD is too subject-specific to allow for training.

I asked for comments on what had been useful and what had not been useful about the courses they had attended. To my surprise (perhaps because I have spent the last four years deliberately putting myself in the way of critical comments about supervisor training), I received a long list of what was (1) useful, and a much shorter list of what was (2) not useful.

Useful

By far the most popular answer, in some shape or form, was the value of '*meeting other supervisors*' and to '*discuss common problems with colleagues*'; it was '*interesting to see how similar problems emerge across different subjects*' and to hear '*about the similar concerns of other supervisor*' and their supervision styles. It saved time, for as one said, training: '*extends experience as it takes a long time to build up if only via individual students*'.

Supervisors talked about the personal gains: '*more confidence in my supervision*'; and a sense of reassurance. '*Learnt new techniques; shared experience; reassurance that I was doing the right thing*'; '*it made me aware of my strengths as a supervisor*'; and '*understanding strengths and areas for improvement*'. Training opened up some of the mysteries of university life:

> It gave me space to think about teaching at this level before I did it, to talk with others and reflect on this. The most useful part was the observations. It is immensely useful to me to see other people teach.
>
> Shared experiences brought to light, and also an idea of what the university expects – not entirely the same as what I did!

This included developing strategies for a variety of situations that might arise:

> It clarified expectations and enabled me to impose some structure to my supervisory practices. It also suggested strategies for dealing with problems.

> Talking with others through examples/case studies of problems that can occur.
> I think by reinforcing what I already half-knew – about prompt feedback,
> encouragement, chasing students up if necessary.
> The workshop was most useful in talking about how to help students pace
> themselves.

Plus, it introduced supervisors to policies and regulations and gave a general overview of the role: *'Rules, protocols and practices'*; *'legal requirements / university procedure and protocol / trouble shooting / sharing with others / case studies / best practice'*; *'it made me aware of the new regulations and their interpretation in my Faculty'*; *'Overview of general problems and procedures'*; and *'Alignment with emerging university/QAA protocols'.* Others were a mix of all these, for example: *'Provided useful information. Allowed me to compare my understanding with that of other supervisors'*; *'Some general principles and discussing issues with other supervisors;* and it made me *'think more about the relationship between student and supervisor and co-supervisors'.*

Not useful

They were invited to comment on what had *not* been useful on courses attended, and where 85 per cent offered positive comments, only 40 per cent made negative ones. A large group found the subject of supervision too diverse so courses attended were too general and superficial, plus the conceptualization of what constitutes PhD study was narrow (e.g. focusing on full-time students only or not recognizing the place of professional doctorates). One commented on the need for hands-on experience to inform courses,

> Of course there is a sense in which supervision is unique and the programme cannot pretend to describe every possible variation. Experience of a number of doctoral candidates and their idiosyncrasies is essential.

A number found the time available too limited to get to the heart of the matter or to genuinely relate to their experience and had to be placed in a wider developmental experience:

> While both were helpful neither really get to the heart of the experience. I have found informal support from my mentor and through joint supervision with him to be very helpful.

Two commented that courses had come late in their supervisory careers and so added little. Three found the content irrelevant: one found there was '*too much general waffling about the student-supervisor relationship*'; and two found it '*patronising*', which one explained as being about reaching university targets rather than about how to supervise.

Experienced staff

Throughout the project people had told me that experienced supervisors resisted training. At first I attached the word 'bewildered' to the tone of experienced supervisors' responses when I asked them about the role of training. With time, as I completed more interviews, I changed 'bewildered' to 'perplexed': perplexed about which aspects of their varied and long careers in research could be selected out and packaged in training and development workshops by non-specialists. This was less, then, about resistance and more questioning how this lifetime of research could possibly be summarized in hints and tips for supervision. One summarized a view of the place of training:

> I have absolutely no idea, since I have never been! I've sort of done a bit of supervisor training with junior colleagues who I've supervised with, but that is more craft training, on the job. I have no idea what you could say in an abstract way, I suppose you do problem issues and so on. I mean, getting a bunch of older and younger supervisors around the table and there being a few good lessons, I could see that could be quite good. I would be hopeless at going to a course and some bod from personnel services telling me how to be a good supervisor.

Others had experienced more cross-faculty meetings and were aware of changing times, seeing a place for specific pieces of information about institutional practices:

> Even something which is just a session of an hour or so maybe to point up some of these things. Yes, more recently, I suppose, I discovered a little bit about how things are done in other faculties and other people emphasising much more the idea of writing draft chapters and of having more of a formal [review] process. In this department there's not been any department guidance about these things . . . I suppose I felt I'd got a way of doing which seemed to work but some of the departmental processes are now a bit different and so the problem is how one engages with all that.

With something as complex as supervision it is hard to disentangle what has been an influence and what one knew at different points in time. Knowledge, once absorbed, becomes expressed as *doing*. Hence, it is hard sometimes to look back and know precisely the impact of courses attended:

> I have attended and even organized such training sessions in the past, but to be honest I really can't remember what they were about. I don't remember that I learned anything from them beyond the obvious thing that everybody says, which is that it is quite good to talk to other supervisors about how they do things, there is not enough of that – there aren't really opportunities for doing that.

Experience brings opportunity to take part in a variety of teaching activities (as teacher or participant) over the years and they are of variable quality:

> We had training courses organized, and I drew this cartoon drawing of a granny being taught to suck eggs, because this kind of young guy had been brought in, he didn't know what he was talking about and it wasn't just a waste of time it actually de-motivated people. Unfortunately I think it's wrong to believe that anyone has got the total sum knowledge of good skills, practice, ideas and everything. I like reading books about things that might suggest new ideas or talking to people – I'll happily go to them, but I do think that it has got to avoid the danger of thinking there is an obligation to put on a training, we'll rope in somebody who will stand up and talk.

So to achieve any level of credibility, awareness and care is needed over who teaches supervision courses, how they are conducted and where course designers expect the boundaries of their knowledge to lie.

Reconstruction

My view now is that courses are best when used to try to influence aspects of supervision and to contribute at different points in the supervisors' career cycle. My aim nowadays is to influence academic practices by providing supervisors with opportunities to help themselves to become more fully aware of the issues surrounding supervision, and to position themselves constructively (their specific styles, hopes, expectations, disciplinary demands, worries, rewards) within that context.

My ideal is to combine courses with assessment exercises that connect the generalities of the course to the reality of supervision; coupled with mentoring in the early stages of a supervisory career from a more experienced colleague in the subject specialism. Courses and accreditation need to align with the supervisor's working situation, with assessments drawing on reflection within the work context as well as demonstrating a wider knowledge of current supervisory matters. It is assessment that provides a bridge between generalist courses and the highly specific elements in a supervisor's disciplinary and departmental context.

Assessment requires supervisors to register and engage with a course. In many ways, this is easier for new supervisors for whom supervision modules may fit into existing systems. For example, they can be attached to the teaching development qualifications that new academics are likely to take. Throughout all of this, of course, are funding and workload allocation implications if mentoring and engagement in colleagues' development are to be taken seriously. Introductions to supervision need to be staged and supported: in many universities, this is now achieved by a junior colleague engaging in supervisory teams which they cannot lead until accreditation and appropriate levels of experience are attained. While not mentorship in the traditional sense, supervisory teams can – when working well – provide supervisors with experience as well as providing students with enriched support. In traditional laboratory and science teams, the model of post-doctoral researchers providing supervision under the direction of the research director is a form of supervisory team but this is a difficult model to transfer to other disciplines.

By now the ingredients of supervision courses are becoming clearer. Courses are useful when they take their place within a broader developmental picture, in which the attributes and skills needed to become a researcher and academic are fundamental to a supervisor's knowledge base and positioning within an international disciplinary community. Courses can enhance the development of individuals' academic identities, and useful courses will allow:

- comparative discussion between supervisors across subjects
- time and opportunity to think about a range of issues that may arise
- analysis of supervision by use of experience, literature and through colleagues' knowledge
- time to be saved by exposing supervisors to a variety of ways of thinking that may otherwise only arise if and when they meet students
- input concerning local and national policies, regulations and expectations of supervisors
- allow people to hear new strategies and ideas to those they have previously met.

Least useful was the inevitably generic and general nature of some courses attended. For training and development courses inevitably remain only a part of the story and courses are always unsatisfactory on their own. To make best use of training opportunities, institutions and supervisors need to expect:

- courses to use participants' experience via constructive and structured reflection
- assessed courses to provide assignments that connect supervisors' reflections to their specific work experience
- departments, schools and faculties to consider mentoring systems
- departments, schools and faculties to provide new supervisors with staged and supported entry to supervision
- to provide a general tool to support continued reflection on supervisory practice for all supervisors
- courses to be understood within the context of allied skills and developments needed for the whole academic career, e.g. as a researcher leading teams, publishing, project management, coaching and training, teaching and lecturing, becoming an examiner, engaging in university committees, subject area national and international activities, and mentoring colleagues.

For educational developers and for supervisors, designing appropriate courses means a pedagogic balancing act that manages awareness and demands arising from competing tensions:

- students' needs, the quality of their research education and experience, and potentially difficult areas, e.g. the division of responsibility for the PhD between students and supervisors
- the reality of supervisors' lives
- institutions' needs
- managers' expectations of what courses do
- external pressures, e.g. funding bodies
- the imperatives of knowledge construction and disciplinary standards.

For trainers, life can sometimes feel like one is sitting in the middle of a firing range, and maintaining confidence in curriculum decisions made some time ago is not always easy. Rather than 'changing with the wind' in response to each set of course participants' comments, I decided to take a far more public route with course design. While course feedback forms keep me in touch with the detail of how material is received and how workshops are structured, the overall shape and direction of courses provided has been unpicked and re-sewn through numerous committees and inspections. One set were internal: to develop a Diploma in Academic Practice module at Master's level, my materials were steered through a variety of local committees. Given that members of different panels had not attended my courses, I have been obliged to defend my thinking, take notice of where it does not make sense to informed readers, weigh up advice and make adjustments. Similarly, I wanted to know how my thinking (especially the actual teaching methods used) aligned with work outside my home university, so I turned to developing my courses so that they could be accredited by the Staff and Educational Development Association (www.seda.ac.uk/).

A part of my wish in providing a SEDA module is that more experienced staff, perhaps those less adept at negotiating teaching development courses than their newer colleagues, might be tempted to try an accredited course. One element I have retained against all the evidence is the right for staff to attend workshops as a 'one-off', without registering for any qualification. Over the years, many experienced supervisors have attended my one-day workshops and they bring with them a wealth of understanding that changes the whole nature of a day. Although not engaging with assessment means that workshops may feel too general to supervisors, nonetheless I like the idea that experienced staff in particular can try a day without further commitment. Plus, should anyone find it relevant or useful, they have opportunities to engage in accreditation.

Workshops and courses

Course organizers may view themselves as trainers or developers, both of which words are laden with assumptions about how to design and teach courses. Participants may be reluctant or happy to attend, expect 'handy hints and tips' specific to their subject area, or be able to make use of generic, cross-disciplinary discussions. Others may be frustrated by the generic nature of courses or hold different conceptualizations of supervision to co-participants and trainers and struggle to position themselves constructively with course material.

There is tension surrounding the words 'training' and 'developing'. For those who dislike the word training, it implies a known body of knowledge transmitted in a way reminiscent of old-style animal training – the trainer is centre-stage, equipped with chairs and whistles, ensuring compliance rather than pedagogic engagement. For those who dislike the word development, it implies woolly, non-specific chatting and group activities that get nowhere in relation to the practical problems that have to be tackled. For those who *like* the word training, it communicates a crispness of knowledge to be transmitted and skills to be taught; and for those who *like* 'development' it gives a sense of the complexity of pedagogy and the need to work with the diversity that participants bring to a course. I am closer to the development end of the continuum: supervision, to me, is too complex and supervisors too varied in achievement to be amenable to 'expert transmission'. However, there are elements (such as local guidelines and local policies) which are easier to transmit, albeit hard for supervisors to work out how to use constructively in their specific circumstances. I am less concerned about the precise vocabulary used concerning training and development than I am about the content and impact of courses, their usefulness in the wider educational scheme of life in universities.

I face the problems all educational developers face: short courses allow a range of people time to attend and pick up some thoughts from colleagues, as well as time to sort out their own ideas. But short courses are superficial, especially if they align only with a 'handy hints and tips' model. Hints and tips can have their place, but it is rare that the right advice is given to people who want it at precisely the moment in their careers that they can use it. Longer courses allow supervisors to engage in-depth with material, but cater only to those who are highly committed and prepared to spend amounts of time, hence excluding those who might only have time or funds for shorter sessions. Treading the line between superficiality and access is a constant balancing act.

Like the trainer quoted in Chapter 5, I too have experienced a distinct generational difference in attitudes about teaching development courses, although I am not completely clear whether this represents age or stage of entry to academe. I have, for example, met staff entering universities later in life who attend supervisor courses in a matter-of-fact manner, transferring from workplaces where updating and training are a standard part of the work environment. For those used to the idea that attending teaching courses is essential rather than voluntary, it is highly likely that they can use shorter courses as part of a wider developmental programme – running alongside reflection on and development of their practice. But even for those who use training in this constructive way, short courses still run the risk of making supervision sound too clear-cut, without a sense of the danger and risk inherent in the PhD which can take both student and supervisor to the edge of their capabilities. Presenting the riskiness of the PhD in short sessions can sound over-dramatic and off-putting as, indeed, to present long case studies full of problems can do too.

Sometimes courses include people who behave unhelpfully. Humility and combativeness do not sit well together, and successful academics do need to be good at arguing. But it is more than skill at arguing alone that can be disruptive: occasionally one meets colleagues who just cannot cope with being taught within the institution in which they work and teach. While this may show itself in any professional development activity, it can be intensified in the realm of doctoral supervision by a fear that control of supervision has slipped away and that the last bastion of true academe – research and scholarship – appears to have been captured by bureaucrats who understand it least. The resulting frustration, given the inevitable limitations of supervisory courses, make for a heady brew, allowing it to seem reasonable to take out on educational developers a range of discontents to do with the frameworks currently surrounding supervision.

Course designers (for both student and supervisor courses) juggle pragmatism with awareness of complexity, needing to move between down-to-earth information one minute, and reflection at depth in the next. Supervisors who contributed to this project showed themselves committed and concerned about the quality of their supervisory work. The notion of a collegial, collaborative style of supervision is still a strong one, although sometimes struggling to adjust to tight timeframes and absorbing new technologies as tools for working with students working at a distance. People's supervision styles developed experientially over time: as part of a supervisor's academic identity it springs from their relationship with research and research communities, positioning supervision as part of extending the boundaries of disciplinary knowledge and understanding. The primacy of subject matter in supervision is mediated through this creative collaboration (at its best) with students. However, this makes supervision and the PhD challenging: not just intellectually, but emotionally and socially. For students, getting a PhD is much more than just acquiring a list of new skills, it is a transformational form of education in which the journey to becoming an independent researcher calls on their qualities of resilience, independence and perseverance as well as cognitive abilities.

Implications for supervision

- Courses cannot teach you all you need to know about supervision, it is too complex a job. To make best use of courses (especially short ones) requires participants to take what is on offer and put in some extra work on reflection, taking time and effort to apply it to their specific circumstances. No one course can be designed to fit one person's requirements absolutely. Self-monitoring allows participants to take control of the process and to reflect on their own knowledge and needs at any moment in time, looking for ways of strengthening their skills and understanding where necessary.

Implications for supervision—Cont'd

- Courses cannot be specific to the myriad variety of PhDs and disciplinary contexts. Participants are the experts in their disciplines and so need to use the non-specific, non- disciplinary nature of most courses as a sounding board to work out what are the relevant questions and solutions in their corner of the academic universe. It is easier for course designers to engage the details of participants' working lives systematically where they engage with assessment. Assignments can tie the specifics of supervisors' immediate work challenges and disciplinary area with the generalities of supervision courses.
- Supervisors pick and hone skills and knowledge at different points in their careers. What is obvious to one person is news to their colleagues. If courses present something you are already skilled in – work out when and how you developed that part of your repertoire. This awareness will improve your mentoring of students and newer supervisors. There are a range of allied approaches to teaching that can inform supervision, such as coaching, mentoring and counselling,
- While many are in agreement that new supervisors should go on some form of training or developmental course, opinion is shifting with regard to more experienced supervisors. No longer is it the case that they are universally seen as resistant to attendance at courses, and indeed, many do attend sessions to update, refresh and to learn about changed agendas. Like new staff, more experienced staff can make better use of courses if they examine their expectations: for courses can, at best, influence thinking about key stages in the supervisory cycle and cannot teach 'everything you need to know about supervision'.

So where does my journey leave me? With a recognition of the power of experiential learning in teaching development, especially when used with intelligent awareness; a preference for designing my own materials and the flexibility to alter them according to the needs of the group I am working with; a reluctance to declaim my own knowledge in places where I want course participants to develop or acknowledge their own understanding; and a confirmation that carefully gathered and sifted information can support course design.

It has brought recognition, too, that in learning to juggle the risks of such a compelling and creative enterprise as the PhD, supervisors and students can benefit from stepping back and attempting to understand their study in a wider frame. The 'flexi-structures' talked about by experienced supervisors interviewed in this project combined the detailed obsession of all researchers about their subject matter with an understanding of pathways through the PhD. If I were transported back to being a PhD student in the light of what I know now, I would attend every course available, to make sense of such pathways alongside the content of my study. Such courses may not have changed the research project itself, but could have illuminated the process that I was engaged with as a student. It is a paradox how confusion about pathways can add to the messy, frustrating, even alarming elements of the PhD and supervision; while a reflective, informed awareness has the potential to release the joy and satisfaction that can come from the creative enterprise of research.

References

Ahern, K. and Manathunga, C. (2004), Clutch-Starting Stalled Research Students. *Innovative Higher Education*, 28 (4), 237–54.

Amundsen, C. and McAlpine, L. (2009), '"Learning supervision": trial by fire'. *Innovations in Education and Teaching International*. 46 (3), 331–42.

Annan, N. (1999), *The Dons: Mentors, Eccentrics and Geniuses*. London: Harper Collins.

Bartlett, A. and Mercer, G. (eds) (2001), *Postgraduate Supervision: Transforming (R)Elations*. New York: Peter Lang.

Bendix Petersen, E. (2007), 'Negotiating academicity: postgraduate research supervision as category boundary work.' *Studies in Higher Education*, 32 (4), 475–87.

Boucher, C. and Smyth, A. (2004), 'Up close and personal: reflections on our experience of supervising research candidates who are using personal reflective techniques.' *Reflective Practice 5(3)*, 345–56.

Bourdieu, P. and Passeron, J. C. (1990), *Reproduction in Education*. London: Sage.

Cameron, J. (1995), *The Artist's Way: a spiritual path to higher creativity*. London: Pan Books.

Cohen, L., Manion, L. and Morrison, K. (2007) *Research Methods in Education*. Sixth edn. Routledge: London.

Crème, P. and Lea, M. R. (2003), *Writing at University: a guide for students*. Second edn. Maidenhead: Open University Press.

Cribb, A. and Gewirtz, S. (2006), 'Doctoral student supervision in a managerial climate'. *International Studies in Sociology of Education*. 16 (3), 223–36.

de Beer, M. & Mason, Roger B. (2009), 'Using a blended approach to facilitate postgraduate supervision'. *Innovations in Education and Teaching International*, 46 (2), May, 213–26.

Delamont, S., Parry, O. and Atkinson, P. (1997), 'Critical Mass and Pedagogic Community: studies in academic habitus.' *British Journal of Sociology of Education*, 18 (4), 533–49.

Denicolo, P. (2004), 'Doctoral supervision of colleagues: peeling off the veneer of satisfaction and competence'. *Studies in Higher Education*, 29 (6), 693–707.

Devenish, R, Dyer, S., Jefferson, T, Lord, L. van Leeuwen, S. and Fazakerley, V. (2009), 'Peer-to-peer support: the disappearing work in the doctoral student experience'. *Higher Education Research and Development*. 8 (1), March, 59–70.

Doncaster, K. and Lester, S. (2002), 'Capability and its Development: experiences from a work-based doctorate'. *Studies in Higher Education*. 27 (1), 91–101.

Egan, R., Stockley, D., Brouwer, B., Tripp, D. and Stechyson, N. (2009), 'Relationships between area of academic concentration, supervisory style, student needs and best practices'. *Studies in Higher Education*, 34 (3), 337–45.

Elton, L. and Pope, M. (1989), 'Research Supervision: the value of collegiality'. *Cambridge Journal of Education*, 19 (3), 267–76.

R. Freedman, C. (2003), 'Do Great Economists Make Great Teachers? George Stigler as a Dissertation Supervisor'. *Journal of Economic Education*. Summer, 282–90.

Glaser, B. G and Strauss, A. L. (1967), *The Discovery of Grounded Theory: Strategies for Qualitative Research*. Chicago: Aldine Publishing Company.

Grant, B. (2001), 'Dirty Work: "A Code for Supervision" Read Against the Grain"', in: A. Bartlett and G. Mercer (eds) *Postgraduate Supervision: Transforming (R)Elations*. New York: Peter Lang, pp. 13–23.

Grimston, J. (2010) 'Cuts will force universities to close "hundreds of courses"'. *The Sunday Times*, 3.1.10, 4.

Hakala, J. (2009), 'Socialization of junior researcher in new academic research environments: two case studies from Finland'. *Studies in Higher Education*, 34 (5), 501–16.

Harley, S., Muller-Camen, M. and Collin, A. (2004), 'From academic communities to managed organisations: The implications for academic careers in UK and German universities'. *Journal of Vocational Behavior*, 64, 329–45.

Harris Report (1996), *Review of postgraduate education*. Bristol: Higher Education Funding Council for England.

Heath, T. (2002), 'A Quantitative Analysis of PhD Students' Views of Supervision'. *Higher Education Research and Development*, 21, 1, 41–53.

Higher Education Funding Council for England (HEFCE) (2005), 'PhD Research Degrees: Entry and Completion'. *Issues Paper*. Downloaded 31.03.09. www.hefce.ac.uk/pubs/hefce/2005/05_02/.

Hockey, J. (1996), 'A contractual solution to problems in the supervision of PhD degrees in the UK'. *Studies in Higher Education*, 21(3), 359–73.

Holligan, C. (2005), 'Fact and fiction: a case history of doctoral supervision'. *Educational Research*, 47(3), 267–78.

Hunt, C. (2001), 'Out of the Void: moving from chaos to concepts in the presentation of a thesis'. *Teaching in Higher Education*, 6 (3), 351–67.

Johnston, D. and Strong, T. (2008), 'Reconciling Voices in Writing an Autoethnographic Thesis'. *International Journal of Qualitative Methods*, 7 (3) 48–61.

Kamler, B. and Thomson, P. (2004), 'Driven to abstraction: doctoral supervision and writing pedagogies'. *Teaching in Higher Education*, 9 (2), 195–209.

Kiley, M. (2009), 'Identifying threshold concepts and proposing strategies to support doctoral candidates'. *Innovations in Education and Teaching International*, 46 (3), August, 293–304.

Kulej, G. and Wells, P. (2009), *Postgraduate Research Experience Survey Technical Report*. Higher Education Academy, 21.10.09. www.heacademy.ac.uk/ourwork/supportingresearch/alldisplay?type=resources&newid=ourwork/postgraduate/pres_technical_report&site=York. Downloaded 5.1.10.

Leonard, D. (2001), *A Woman's Guide to Doctoral Studies*. Buckingham: Open University Press.

Leonard, D., Becker, R. and Coate, K. (2004), 'Continuing professional and career development: the doctoral experience of education alumni at a UK university'. *Studies in Continuing Education*, 26 (3), 369–85.

Marton, F. (1981), 'Phenomenography – describing conceptions of the world around us'. *Instructional Science*, 10, 177–200. www.ped.gu.se/biorn/phgraph/misc/constr/phegraph.html. Downloaded 3.1.10.

Marton, F. (1994), 'Phenomenography' in T. Husén and T. N. Postlethwaite (eds), *The International Encyclopedia of Education*. Second edn, Volume 8. Oxford: Pergamon, pp. 4,424–9. Available: www.ped.gu.se/biorn/phgraph/civil/main/1res.appr.html. Downloaded November 2009.

McClellan, A. (2005), 'Clock Ticks on the PhD' *The Independent*. http://license.icopyright.net/user/viewFreeUse.act?fuid=MzA3MjUxOQ%3D%3D. Downloaded 31.03.09.

McCormack, C. (2005), 'Is non-completion a failure or a new beginning? Researching non-completion from a student's perspective'. *Higher Education Research and Development*, 24, 3, 233–47.

McMichael, P. (1993), 'Starting up as supervisors: the perceptions of newcomers in postgraduate supervision in Australia and Sri Lanka'. *Studies in Higher Education*, 18 (1), 15–27.

Meyer, J. H. F. and Land, R. (eds) (2006), *Overcoming barriers to student understanding: Threshold concepts and troublesome knowledge*. Abingdon, UK: Routledge.

Morley, L., Leonard, D., and David, M. (2002), 'Variations in Vivas: quality and equality in British PhD assessments'. *Studies in Higher Education*, 27, (3), 263–73.

Office of the Independent Adjudicator for Higher Education (2005), *Annual Report*. www.oiahe.org.uk. Downloaded August 2007.

Park, C. (2005), 'The New Variant PhD: The changing nature of the doctorate in the UK'. *Journal of Higher Education Policy and Management*, 27 (2), 189–207.

Park, C. (2007) 'Redefining the Doctorate'. *Higher Education Academy Discussion Paper*. January 2007. www.heacademy.ac.uk/assets/York/documents/ourwork/research/redefining_the_doctorate.pdf. Downloaded 3/1/10.

Pearce, L. (2005), *How to Examine a Thesis*. Open University Press: Maidenhead.

Peelo, M. (1994), *Helping Students with Study Problems*. Buckingham: SRHE/Open University Press.

Peelo, M. (2002), 'Struggling to Learn', in M. Peelo and T. Wareham (eds), *Failing Students in Higher Education*. SRHE/Open University Press: Buckingham, pp. 160–71.

Pole, C. and Sprokkereef, A. (1997), 'Supervision of doctoral students in the natural sciences: expectations and experiences'. *Assessment and Evaluation in Higher Education*. 22 (1), 49–64.

Quality Assurance Agency (2004), *Code of Practice*. www.qaa.ac.uk/academicinfrastructure/codeOfPractice/default.asp

Rapoport, T., Yair, G. and Kahane, R. (1989), 'Tutorial relations – the dynamic of social contract and personal trust'. *Interchange*, 20, 14–26.

Rudd, E. (1985), *A New Look at Postgraduate Failure*. Guildford, Surrey: SRHE & NFER-Nelson.

Sheskin, D. J. (2004), *Handbook of Parametric and Nonparametric Statistical Procedures*. Third edn. Boca Raton, Florida: Chapman & Hall/CRC.

Silverman, D. (2005), *Doing Qualitative Research*. Second edn. London: Sage.

Sinclair, S. (1997), *Making Doctors: an institutional apprenticeship*. London: Berg.

Styles, I. and Radloff, A. (2000), 'Jabba the Hut: Research students' feelings about doing a thesis', in Hermann, A. and Kulski, M. M. (eds), *Flexible Futures in Tertiary Teaching*. Proceedings of the 9th Annual Teaching Forum, 2–4 February 2000. Perth: Curtin University of Technology. http://lsn.curtin.edu.au/tlf/tlf2000/contents.html. Downloaded 7.10.09.

Swales, J. M. (1990), *Genre Analysis: English in academic and research settings*. Cambridge: Cambridge University Press.

Taylor, S. and Beasley, N. (2005), *A Handbook for Doctoral Supervisors*. Abingdon: Routledge.

Tinkler, P. and Jackson, C. (2004), *The Doctoral Examination Process*. Maidenhead: Open University.

Torrance, M. S. and Thomas, G.V. (1994), 'The Development of Writing Skills in Doctoral Research Students'. Chapter 6 in: Robert E. Burgess (ed.), *Postgraduate Education and Training in the Social Sciences: Processes and Products*. London: Jessica Kingsley.

Trafford, V. and Leshem, S. (2008), *Stepping Stones to Achieving your Doctorate: by focusing on your viva from the start*. Maidenhead: Open University Press McGraw Hill.

Trafford, V. and Leshem, S. (2009), 'Doctorateness as a threshold concept'. *Innovations in Education and Teaching International*, 46 (3), 305–16.

Vilkinas, T. (2008), 'An Exploratory Study of the Supervision of PhD/Research Students' Theses.' *Innovation in Higher Education*, 32, 297–311.

Whitelock, D., Faulkner, D. and Miell, D. (2008), 'Promoting creativity in PhD supervision: Tensions and dilemmas'. *Thinking Skills and Creativity*, 3, 143–53.

Williams, M. (2002), 'Generalization in interpretive research', in Tim May (ed.), *Qualitative research in action* (pp.125–43). London: Sage.

Wisker, G., Robinson, G., Trafford, V., Warnes, M. and Creighton, E. (2003), 'Dialogues to Successful PhDs: strategies supporting and enabling the learning conversations of staff and students at post-graduate level'. *Teaching in Higher Education*. 8 (3), 383–97.

Wisker, G and Robinson, G. (2009), 'Encouraging postgraduate students of literature and art to cross conceptual thresholds'. *Innovations in Education and Teaching International*. 46 (3), 317–30.

Woodhouse, M. (2002), 'Supervising dissertation projects: expectations of supervisors and students'. *Innovations in Education and Teaching International*, 39 (2), 137–42.

Wright, T. and Cochrane, R. (2000), 'Factors Influencing Successful Submission of PhD Theses'. *Studies in Higher Education*, 25 (2), 181–95.

Index